THE PATH OF A WOUNDED HEALER

LIBERATION IS FOR THE ASKING

Sara Bachmeier

Author's Tranquility Press
Atlanta, Georgia

Sara Bachmeier/Author's Tranquility Press
3800 Camp Creek Parkway, SW building 1400-116, #1255
Atlanta, GA 30331
www.authorstranquilitypress.com

Ordering Information:
Quantity sales. Special discounts are available on quantity purchases by corporations, associations, and others. For details, contact the "Special Sales Department" at the address above.

The Path of a Wounded Healer/Sara Bachmeier
Paperback: 978-1-959579-79-3
eBook: 978-1-959579-80-9

White Raven lives now

In this precious golden moment,

Casting light into the darkness of the night.

White Raven transforms each precious moment of being—

Every breath is a gift,

Golden in its nature.

Bringing rebirth, renewal, recovery, reflection, and healing,

White Raven reveals the source of eternal joy

Emanating from within.

Table of Contents

PREFACE

To thine own self be true.

—Shakespeare

"To thine own self be true" is a mantra that I have been hearing a lot lately. But what does this mean?

To me, this statement leads toward self-love. If we are old souls, protectors of the earth, speakers of truth, guardians of the animals, seekers of enlightenment, light warriors, believers in equality, light workers, or starseeds, the odds were against us from the very beginning.

We did not incarnate into a world of acceptance, peace, and understanding.

Most likely, we felt alone and misunderstood, and what appeared to be normal for everyone else around us felt like a hostile and foreign environment.

Trying to fit into a society that we do not recognize goes against the grain of our beloved inner truth. It is like wearing clothes that are too tight or out of style. It just does not feel good or right. As we try expressing ourselves and building lives of authenticity, we are considered reclusive, rebellious, and possibly dangerous to the outside world.

We finally come to a fork in the road. To the left, we choose to honor ourselves at the cost of being outcasts, or we turn to the right, where we pretend to be individuals we are not and slowly build inner resentment for which our hearts will eventually pay a price.

To those of us who have embraced the left path, we have chosen to live by a code of honor— "To thine own self be true." It is not the most popular route by any means, but it is the beginning of true self-love.

It is the way of authenticity and where our creative energies are conceived.

This is the land of the dreamer and where the bridge to the outer realms appears. It is our homeland and the passageway to freedom.

Once we ground ourselves with acceptance, we begin to comprehend that we are the messengers, bringers of light and truth, the courageous ones, bowing before no human, religion, or society.

Personally, we live through the means of love for human values; we are defenders of nature and her elements, servants only to inner peace.

There may be only a few of us, but individually, we are all connected by a rainbow spectrum woven together through the promise to always be true to ourselves, and this is our key to salvation as we forge along to become the captains of our ships and the winds at our sails.

INTRODUCTION

Once we reach the fifth dimension, we are out of the woods from the limiting confines of perceiving the world in terms of good and bad and being subjected to the polarities of judgment.

In this dimension, our higher hearts are linked with the pineal gland, also known as the third eye, activating the opening of our crown chakras, and when our crown chakras are open, it represents the stage in our lives when we are self-realized. No longer depending on the polarities of male or female, human or divine, we understand the physical reality as but one small segment of our total selves. We come to the realization that our choice to incarnate during this space and time is to fulfill our mission and reason for embodiment.

When this happens, we dissolve our need to judge the world and awaken the feeling of connection to all life, knowing we are all One.

My first book, *Egyptian Numerology: Emergence into the Fifth Dimension*, may have come a little before its time, but the veils between worlds have been lifting, relieving us from the separation of birth-amnesia, allowing us to remember who we are and why we came here. During this process, there is a need for guidance, inspiration, or paths to take. The book was written to explore, expand, and raise our consciousness into the fifth-dimension reality so we can access our higher possibilities and probabilities. I describe in detail the path I took evolving into a higher realm to channel the number definitions and characteristics found in part 2 of the book. Very few individuals are ready to take this leap, but for those who have been waiting for this information, this book is a transformational guide.

Another controversial subject regarding my books is the mention of the word *God*. People are obsessed with labels when it comes to identifying religious preferences, and this leads to the separation between people. I believe in a higher power, but I disregard the need, or desire, to assign an identity to it. I believe in love, light, and unity, regardless of spiritual beliefs, and whether I choose to call it God, Source, Great Universe, Buddha, or Divine Energy, it is of no consequence to me. Some people are unwilling to overlook their prejudices to find true wisdom and what resonates deeply within their hearts because they see this powerful word and, for internal reasons, struggle.

I use various terms interchangeably to refer to a higher power. Both books recognize the sacred mysteries as my eyes, ears, and heart open to the wisdom, beauty, and miracles surrounding me daily, and this ignites my soul beyond words.

"I say Namaste because I love what it means and not because I am Hindu. A lot of people believe I am a Christian because they hear me speak of Christian values and the truth is, I voice Human values. I have been asked if I am a Buddhist because I have discovered inner peace. Many of my friends are pagans and believe I am one too because I say that being in nature is like going to temple. Do you want to know who I really Am? It is amazingly simple; I do not need a label to define myself because I am a piece of the Universe, sentient, unfractured, and manifested. I Am Awake." (anonymous)

I would like to express my gratitude to all sentient beings who have taken up the courage, self-love, and torch to excavate the light hidden beneath the amnesia of their souls. *The Path of a Wounded Healer: Liberation Is for the Asking* is a sequel to my first book. It describes in greater detail the challenges, blessings, lessons, and teachings I have endured and learned to integrate while traveling on my intended path, purpose, and destiny in this incarnation.

There are specific numerology calculations we choose to be born into that determine why our lives have taken the twists and turns we call struggles. My hope is to help people understand that nothing is random, and everything has purpose and reason. Once I understood the value of my soul-life agreement, I found peace and determination strong enough to go beyond human limitations and conditions and heal some of the hardest challenges a human will ever have to face.

PART I

<u>CHAPTER 1</u>

Egyptian Numerology

*Egyptian numerology is the alchemy of ancient wisdom,
frequencies of numbers, and position of the planets transforming
our lives toward prosperity, love, and overall well-being.
Working with the magical resonance of numbers transmutes
lead into gold as challenges melt into pivotal opportunities.*

Egyptian numerology does not compete with traditional numerology. Its purpose is to extend, expand, and elevate the next step beyond traditional numerology. If you have taken basic numerology as far as you can go and are hungry for more, Egyptian numerology opens doors and perspectives beyond the three-dimensional view of positive and negative concepts found within the vibrational forces of number frequencies.

Through my research and understanding, I introduce a divining tool linked to the philosophy and teachings of Pythagoras, historically known as the Father of Numerology because of his profound discovery of the natural bond between number frequencies and the human psyche.

He taught us that all life is understood through the frequencies of numbers and discovered the correlation between life existing in nature and the vibrations of numbers. He used this interconnection to transcend the meaning of life.

He discovered that every number vibration holds a unique personality, characteristic, and potential, each of which is connected to nature and observed through our senses. This includes the stars, moon, sun, planets, seasons, elements, sounds, textures, colors, flavors, scents, and even animals. Everything is made of energy, and the study of numbers is a tool we use to digest the sacred ancient truths of the universe through our sixth sense.

Pythagoras demonstrated how combining elements that resonate at specific number frequencies enhanced a desired outcome and established sacred initiations, thereby establishing the virtues of each number vibration. His initiates followed and practiced these twelve initiations as they sought self-realization and enlightenment.

The veils of density and birth amnesia separating the spirit world from humanity have been thinning over the past several decades, and ancient wisdom is being unearthed from many cultures around the world. We know these truths by listening to our hearts and trusting our intuition.

We are no longer bound to churches and religions to advance our spiritual directives. When utilizing number frequencies to their fullest potential, we must know that everything is connected and be willing to open our minds to the vault of knowledge available to us.

My first book, *Egyptian Numerology: Emergence into the Fifth Dimension*, was originally written to accompany me as an instruction booklet for when I teach classes and workshops. It delves into the importance of raising our vibrations to tap into the higher qualities offered by number frequencies. In that book, I list corresponding properties and give examples of elements that vibrate and resonate to each number. I explain how Egyptian numerology, when combined with the law of attraction, can help us maximize our personal development and achieve our desires by raising our spirits, energies, or vibrations to align with the number frequencies in our birth and name charts. I give specific details of techniques I have used to discover the secret realms and doorways of higher consciousness. There are references to how all life is connected to number frequencies and not just limited to characteristic and personality types. By choosing to implement other elements in our use of numbers, we open our imaginations to the highest form of creativity and manifestation. We raise our vibrations by lifting our spirits through action, bringing us to joy, happiness, and peace, or we create an elevated vibe by practicing disciplines that ramp up our energy levels, including meditation, chanting, yoga, exercise, breath work, singing, and composing. These are only a few activities that offer us this natural high.

The Path of the Wounded Healer: Liberation Is for the Asking is a sequel to my first book, and it focuses on the importance of the challenges we face in life. There are specific number frequencies we choose to be born under that influence our emotional maturity. Once I understood that my traumas in life were predetermined and in alignment with the path I have chosen to take in life, it helped me perceive the bigger picture that I do not always have access to. It encouraged me to accept my trials and tribulations with honor, stirred my devotion to always seek my truth, and advised me with answers to some of the toughest questions:

- Why do bad things happen to good people?
- If there is a God, why do so many innocent animals and people suffer?
- Why isn't life fair?

- What happens to people who do not heal their wounds?
- What is the significance of remembering a past life?
- What is the meaning of the fifth dimension?

Living in Alignment

While Egyptian numerology's primary focus is on numbers, those who study with me know that to access our highest possibilities, an evolution in consciousness *must* take place.

In the process of raising our awareness, we are perceptive to signs, symbols, and synchronicities in nature—like number sequencing. We learn to see, hear, feel, and sense other realms because they are doorways into a greater understanding of the dimensions around us.

Our souls crave connection, and we are ultimately pulled in countless directions throughout our lives. What causes our attraction to specific people, places, things, events, and circumstances? Is it random, or are there underlining forces within and outside of us at play?

Egyptian numerology believes that we all made a contract or agreement in the spirit realm with our guides and angels to achieve specific goals, learn certain lessons, and be of service to humankind. This contract is decoded in the numerology of our birth dates and names. These agreements come with an enormous amount of detail. We all have two guides, or angels, that support us and help keep us on track. One is called the *timekeeper*, and the other is the *record keeper*.

The timekeeper ensures all people, places, things, events, and circumstances are orchestrated and met on time. The timekeeper works with life cycles, including the stars, moon, sun, planets, and seasons. The record keeper organizes all our affairs and details, including appointments we make, messages and information we receive, books we read, and important chance meetings we have with others.

We set up timelines (cycles) and circumstances to occur in our lifetimes, and these guides are with us to make sure everything runs according to our plans. This is part of our akashic records, and all this information is in our special book.

We set up *everything* before we are born, including when we are born, where we are born, what family we are born into, what education and religion we are subjected to, our hereditary illnesses, biology, and culture. We come into this lifetime to undergo specific challenges, clear past karma, learn vital lessons, or teach others.

Can we change the plans once we get here? Absolutely! We are born with free will and can choose to ignore the opportunities we have previously assigned to ourselves. Are there consequences? Absolutely! We are given several chances to get back on track once we miss our marks, but ultimately, our lessons and lives will not make sense to us if we reject the paths we have previously laid out to follow. Our lives will just feel off, and we may become restless, irritable, and depressed.

No matter what we choose, our soul learns from every experience, even though the journey back home may take a longer route. There is nothing wasted because ultimately our soul uses every experience for our advancement, and in time, all is used for our highest good.

Being in alignment with our soul-life agreement is a natural wonder. It is compared to the feeling one has when bowling a strike, winning a marathon, hitting the bull's-eye on the dartboard, winning the lottery, holding twenty-one in blackjack, or striking the target at the rifle range. But the feeling of being in alignment with our soul-life agreements is not a momentary elation. This feeling of euphoria is induced within us every morning when we open our eyes, accompanies us throughout the day, visits every decision we make with confidence, and kisses us gently when we go to sleep at night.

Our soul wants to be in alignment and will send clues and nudges when we struggle to find that balance. Unfortunately, sometimes when we manifest wrong turns, we find ourselves experiencing divorce, unemployment, illness, and depression.

The universe, angels/guides, and our higher selves use all means necessary to lead us back to alignment with our soul life agreement because in essence, these are our road maps, our GPS, and our North Stars to what makes sense to us vibrationally. There are obvious signs we witness when we are in or out of alignment with our sacred treaties.

Signs of Being out of Alignment

- fear about the future
- procrastination
- addiction
- anxiety
- depression
- insomnia
- guilt
- low esteem
- lack of motivation
- illness
- resentment
- worry about finances
- fatigue
- self-centered behavior

- complaints and unhappiness
- anger and disappointment

Signs of Being in Alignment

- security and passion about the future
- confidence
- emotional, physical, mental, social, and spiritual balance
- inner peace
- lucid dreaming
- light work
- clear chakras
- personal power and boundaries
- a feeling of being present
- forgiveness
- acceptance
- health/energy
- resourcefulness
- manifest abundance
- generosity
- bliss

Becoming aligned is not a goal but rather a by-product of right living. Spiritual fitness is a conscious choice we make daily. What we think, do, and say determines a whole series of events. If we lack clarity, direction, and understanding with our purpose in life, we risk becoming distracted and falling out of alignment with our soul-life mission.

Being and staying true to our soul-life agreement is possible and achievable. We are changing lives every day.

CHAPTER 2

Bridge over Turbulent Waters

There will come a time when you will lose everything, including your mind. Once you have lost your mind, you will be left with nothing but your soul and this is when you will know that you are invincible.

—Daniel Saint

The information I teach is an accumulation of knowledge obtained from a course I took with Dr. Sharon Forest. After completing the course, I spent a year of independent study and research about the meaning of numbers along with developing my channeling abilities. I use my gift of inner knowing (*clairomniscience*) to determine whether the information I receive is correct. I have a diverse group of spirit guides that channel through me while I am preparing to write. The most consistent is Ascended Master Kuthumi, to whom I dedicate the history of Egyptian numerology. His incarnation as Pythagoras gives him a special interest in this subject, and his soul's evolution as a wounded healer is of internal value and creditworthy.

Being a wounded healer is not a path for everyone. Why do some souls choose this path? In Egyptian numerology, there are specific numbers that carry the path of a wounded healer in their numerology charts. Although the path of a wounded healer is not isolated to a numeric formula, there are special reasons why individuals choose to be born under the influence of a master number, number 6 and number 9.

Does Pain Have to Be the Touchstone of Spiritual Growth?

In Egyptian numerology, the answer to this question is yes for the fortunate few who carry specific number frequencies in their numerology charts. These individuals have a sojourn quite different from those of the rest of the population. Their path is called a *wounded healer*, and many will experience the journey of the dark night of the soul at least once in their lifetimes. In fact, in Egyptian numerology, there are specific past-life insights to all the numbers, but these distinct individuals incarnated to lift the consciousness of humankind through their unique soul-life agreements.

Egyptian numerology lives under the premise that we all made a contract before birth, to come into this lifetime, achieve specific goals, and walk certain paths, and this information can be decoded through the number frequencies given in our birth dates and names. Under this theory, we chose these specific number vibrations to be born through and all the karmic hardships in our lifetimes so we could overcome these difficulties and help heal the world in qualified areas.

All master numbers are endowed with many powers from within, significant strengths, and many more challenges than other numbers. People with these numbers normally realize early in life that they have the capacity to accomplish a great deal with relatively little effort. They contain superpowers hidden within their numbers and are here to obtain personal power and spiritual evolution and, most of all, to be healers for the wounded through their own personal transformations. They will undergo the difficulties and challenges that only a true spiritual warrior and devotional disciple of higher wisdom could ever dream of combating in one lifetime.

People who carry the frequency of master numbers may experience exceptionally painful, turbulent childhoods and must use these experiences to create a better world because of it and not despite it. If anything, the path of master numbers is more karmic than others because they often must transcend more difficulties than other numbers to excel in the first place. Many are original thinkers and end up working alone or find themselves in a position to defend ideas against a hostile majority. They deal with obstacles that daunt the stoutest of hearts.

A wounded healer is a person who specifically contracted before birth to undergo challenges and hardships that often lead to disabilities, trauma, posttraumatic stress disorder (PTSD), illness, and a period called the *dark night of the soul.* The reasons behind these unpleasant life circumstances are to achieve the vital lessons, come out the other side, gain empathy and compassion to connect with others, and be of service to humankind at a large capacity. By overcoming their challenges, they enter the golden chamber of honor, allowing them to bask in divine light and become a channel for eternal oneness with Source.

Only advanced souls with high spiritual directives choose to be born under these powerful frequencies. Our higher selves, angels, and spirit guides would never allow us to be born under these commanding forces unless convinced that we have the experience, stamina, foresight, and ability to use our potential wisely and for the highest good of all involved.

The true power of these numbers lie in the magic of transformation because when they transmute their challenges, they automatically raise the consciousness of the masses. Energetically and on a collective consciousness level, when one person heals from these experiences, it helps to heal hundreds of thousands of victims still held hostage by their suffering, fears, inner demons, and conflicts. Therefore, it is considered one of the highest honors given to human existence.

Past-life healing and soul awareness let us evolve faster when we heal the wounds that are constantly repeating while moving through this life with more guidance and understanding. That is powerful! In one lifetime, we hold the power to heal hundreds of past, current, and future versions of ourselves. Not only that, but in healing ourselves and breaking patterns, we release our ancestors and children from suffering these patterns and repair the world in the process. This is literally one of the most profound conditions we are all here to accomplish. We are here to awaken to this potentiometer, clear these lives, and birth a new earth—a place where people are raised in love, awareness, healing, and soul. The beginning of our real-life utopia, new earth, and the salvation of humanity always starts with ourselves.

Of course, we are all given free will, and some individuals who carry these frequencies will not always serve the light. As we have found, there are those who have used their powers against the light and caused harm instead of healing, and there are souls who do not make it through the dark night of the soul and choose to terminate their incarnation early.

Some people in the limelight who carry these numbers in their birth charts are Oprah Winfrey, Barack Obama, Charles Manson, Whitney Houston, James Dean, Eckhart Tolle, Louise Hay, Dalai Lama, Adolf Hitler, Wayne Dyer, Joseph Stalin, Neil Diamond, Leonardo da Vinci, Britney Spears, Neil Young, Jim Carrey, Keanu Reeves, Donald Trump, Meryl Streep, Michael Jackson, Mark Twain, Brad Pitt, John Lennon, Bill Gates, and Michelle Obama, to mention only a few.

In my studies, there is no greater example of love bridging over turbulent waters than the soul-life agreement of Pythagoras while serving his many incarnations before finally ascending as Master Kuthumi. He demonstrated the law of grace by transmuting and transporting his pain and suffering into courageous acts of love and compassion for all of humankind. I will share with you three amazing incarnations of one soul illustrating how an individual chooses to transform his or her personal darkness to bring love and light into our world. In these stories lies the history of Egyptian numerology.

The Soul-Life Agreement of Pythagoras

Historically, Pythagoras is known as a Greek philosopher, but we recognize him as an Egyptian sage who, around 570 BCE, established a mystery school and gathered initiates to study the sacred art of mathematics, sacred geometry, and the deeper study of science within the energy of numbers. This school was destined to become the Mystery School for the Great White Brotherhood—the masters of light.

He stated that numbers have personalities, characteristics, strengths, and weaknesses that interrelate with all things in life. He believed that mathematics is the basis for everything, and geometry is the highest form of mathematical studies.

Pythagoras saw, felt, and understood the world through mathematics and knew the physical world through the energy of numbers.

He studied with the Greek philosophers and, after having acquired all that was possible for him to learn, became an initiate in Eleusinian mysteries, went to Egypt, and succeeded in securing initiation in the mysteries of Isis at the hands of the priest of Thebes. He continued to travel through many lands and acquired teachings including Egyptian, Babylonian, and the Chaldean mysteries. Pythagoras was said to be the first man to call himself a philosopher. Before that time, the wise men had called themselves *sages*, which are interpreted as "those who know." Being modest, he preferred the word *philosopher*, which is defined as "one who is attempting to find out."

After wandering and studying, he finally settled and established a school at Crotone, a Dorian colony in Southern Italy. He gathered a small group of sincere disciples instructing them in sacred wisdom, the fundamentals of occult mathematics, music, and astronomy, which he considered to be the triangular foundation of all the arts and science.

As so often the case with a genius, Pythagoras incurred both political and personal enmity because of his outspokenness. At one point during his teachings, he refused initiation to a man who in turn sought revenge by destroying both Pythagoras and his philosophy. By means of false propaganda, the disgruntled man turned the minds of the common people against Pythagoras, and without warning, a band of murderers descended on the small group of buildings where the great teacher and his disciples dwelled, burning the structures, and killing Pythagoras.

As Pythagoras, he lived his life as an original thinker, continued his studies against the hostile majority, and brought to life the esoteric findings of numerology. He was a great man whose teachings and efforts were only to serve and illuminate humankind.

Saint Francis of Assisi

In another incarnation, he served as Saint Francis of Assisi, born 1181 in Assisi, Italy, until his death on October 3, 1226, and is fondly remembered for his love of animals and nature and for his most generous spirit. But Francis experienced the processes of becoming a wounded healer and undergoing the wrath of the dark night of the soul. He was encumbered by dark shadows, to the point that he experienced long periods of anguish and depression during his lifetime. His psychological trauma began with his military service in Assisi's war against its more powerful neighbor, Perugia. He witnessed his childhood friends tortured in a devastating battle, and he was taken prisoner and thrown in a dark, damp hole in the ground for a year.

This left him broken and traumatized. When he returned home from the war, he was too physically and emotionally ill to leave the house until he received a message from God to "rebuild my church." It was at this point that he chose to ride the waves of his pain and suffering while allowing the grace of God to heal his body and mind. He obeyed literally by rebuilding San Damiano and restoring it with his own hands. He rebuilt a church through poverty, chastity, obedience, and evangelical zeal, all motivated through love that bridged over his turbulent waters.

He transmuted his war trauma and dark shadows into entire service toward God, and from his brokenness, Francis found the insights leading him to oppose warfare; promoted an alternative to the greed running rampant in the church; and identified with the poor, lepers, and all the other outcasts. He warned his disciples that when a servant of God gets disturbed about something, he must get up and pray at once because if you delay, staying in the shadows, the sickness will grow and unless scrubbed with tears, it will produce in the heart permanent rust.

Koot Hoomi Lal Singh

His last incarnation before ascension was as Koot Hoomi Lal Singh, nineteenth-century Kashmiri Brahman from Shigatse, Tibet. He studied at universities in Oxford and Germany and in 1875, along with El Morya (also an ascended master), founded the Theosophical Society to reacquaint humankind with the ancient wisdom that underlies all world religions and to ensure that long-lost truths resurface.

Before he became enlightened, he underwent a spell of darkness and spent a couple of years wandering in Europe, suffering from a deep depression and restlessness of the mind. It was during this time that he described his adventure as having to surrender his ego or small mind to liberate his higher consciousness. He admitted that he had to literally lose his mind to gain true perspective. After his journey, he became enlightened and gave us this message:

Refuse to be distracted or thwarted. Use your stubbornness rightly by concentrating only upon that which is good and in that way, you truly overcome evil in every sense of the word. Allow me to show you ways to access the reaches of the higher dimensions where peace is accessible to all. Above the din of the Earth plane, we reach Nirvana together, singly, yet side by side. The holiest prospect is teaching peace through self-attainment.

The soul-life agreement of Pythagoras, Saint Francis, and Koot Hoomi was encumbered with the challenges of a wounded healer, and he certainly walked through the dark night of the soul, but his pure love and willingness to be dedicated to his truth liberated his soul and left us with only a positive and illuminating legacy. He is now known as Ascended Master Kuthumi, having made his ascension in the late 1800s.

Other past lifetimes include Balthazar, one of the Three Wise Men who came to Baby Jesus, and, later, as Shah Jahan, builder of the Taj Mahal.

Ascended Master Kuthumi

Pythagoras presently holds the position as Ascended Master Kuthumi and works directly with earthbound *initiates*. He is the doorkeeper of the ancient mysteries and is also the co-protector of the Holy Grail— known as the ancient quest for true higher self-awareness, which we know today as enlightenment. Master Kuthumi will be instrumental in the reemergence of the ancient higher knowledge and instruction that has been lost to humankind for so long. He also endeavors to encourage all concerned to open our hearts for expression toward unconditional love to all.

"I AM Light" by the Ascended
Master Kuthumi

I AM Light, glowing Light,
Radiating Light, intensified Light.
God consumes my darkness,
Transmuting it into Light.

This day I AM a focus of the Central Sun.
Flowing through me is a crystal river,
A living fountain of Light
That can never be qualified
By human thought and feeling.
I AM an outpost of the Divine.

Such darkness as has used me is swallowed up
By the mighty river of Light which I AM.

I AM, I AM, I AM Light;
I live, I live, I live in Light.
I AM Light's fullest dimension;
I AM Light's purest intention.
I AM Light, Light, Light
Flooding the world everywhere I move,
Blessing, strengthening, and conveying
The purpose of the kingdom of heaven

Egyptian numerology works with Master Kuthumi, giving a vital and fresh perspective to the rising qualities of number frequencies in the new era.

It stems from fifth-dimension answers to ongoing questions asked by soul seekers everywhere. The information is channeled through the heart and bypasses the dualities and projections of our minds.

Egyptian numerology encourages individuals to reach higher than the material world, open our imaginations, and dream the best version of ourselves by not settling for anything that does not support our passions.

It challenges us to awaken and stay awake through investigating signs, symbols, and synchronicity; advance our spiritual directives by aligning our energy centers; and love ourselves through compassion, understanding, and forgiveness.

Authenticity is a sovereign journey that becomes lonely only if our paths are not in alignment with Source. It is an experience of mortal freedom incomparable to anything less than divine.

> The message and vision through Egyptian numerology is to offer individuals an opportunity to view their highest abilities and encourage them to release dreams and possibilities to achieve their greatest potential in this lifetime.

> I embolden people to witness their challenges as opportunities, to serve the greater cause for humankind, and to use love as the ultimate bridge over troubled waters.

CHAPTER 3

Becoming the Miraculous Healer

*In order for the teachings of mystical spirituality to come true
in your life, you must make them the central force in your life.
You must center your life around them and infuse them into
every aspect of your life.*

—The Egyptian Book of the Dead

The Egyptians had mystery schools, and within these various studies were initiations that one had to pass through in order to enter the gates of spiritual awareness. They worked with number frequencies and not only their characteristics but the laws that govern them.

In Egyptian numerology, there are twelve initiations on our path to spiritual awareness. Initiations come to us in the form of virtues. They hold the keys to a higher knowledge, understanding of ourselves, and an acute perception of the world around us.

When we accept the invitation to spiritual awakening, we begin to recognize, practice, and implement them in our daily lives. They become keys to the gates we pass through to a higher understanding of rightful living. Some people are born with an inner sense of higher wisdom, and some of us find them along the path of self-discovery. If we desire to achieve personal attainment, these initiations are stepping- stones to reaching an elevated state of consciousness.

All initiations are acts of personal power. They show up in our lives as opportunities to adopt virtues, and these specific merits hold a high level of energy when implemented in our lives daily.

The reason why we accept these initiations when they are presented to us is because they lead us through gates of spiritual awareness, allowing us to maintain a high-energy status. The higher we vibrate, the greater possibilities we attract into our lives. All gates can be entered independently, or they can be used to build on one another. Every gate interacts with and can be applied to all other gates. The numbers associated with each gate resonate with the vibration and the characteristic of the number frequency assigned to that gate, referring to one's soul-life path number.

The vibrations of our life path numbers have magnetic qualities, attracting specific people, places, events, and circumstances to us, and these circle or orbit our lives in an attempt to bring us opportunities to advance our spiritual directives concerning the meaning found within these initiations, virtues, or lessons. Each of us can go an entire lifetime or more not completing these lessons only to return in attempt to finalize the ascension back home. Learning these qualities and implementing them into our lives is a huge part of being in alignment with our souls' journeys.

Initiations offer an opening to a higher awareness, exclusive opportunities, and a soul revelation. If we find ourselves out of alignment, there is sure to be an initiation that is blocked, or maybe we have been unwilling to accept, implement, and explore the depths of its truth within our lives.

These initiations are doorways, openings, or portals to gates of spiritual awareness. We never access the key to these doors and then graduate. They serve as an abyss of expanded wisdom; like a peeling onion, there is always another layer beneath the surface.

It takes daily vigilance and commitment to hold these virtues and be true to ourselves under all conditions and circumstances. Although this path is under the premise of progress and not perfection, there lies an infinite Tao that longs to be grasped and maintained.

We may know the definitions of each initiation, but how are they understood and practiced in our lives? Are we becoming examples or content to be wanderers?

A wanderer is educated about spiritual awareness but never truly goes through the transformation process required to sustain necessary progress. Wanderers tend to talk a good talk, but their walk is always sideways.

I encourage you to embrace these initiations and embody the chasm of truth within your soul, and in doing so, you will lead others through these doorways and closer to their soul-life missions.

Every soul-life path contains a number frequency with a past-life karmic lesson to impart. When I work with individuals, we cover the alignment of the initiation associated with their soul-life path numbers. Our goal is to strengthen this initiation until it develops into the leading character of our personalities. We then better understand the karmic lessons through the virtues that each number frequency is assigned to.

Life-Path Number Initiations

number 1: Interdependence leading to honesty
number 2: Absolving judgment leading to acceptance
number 3: Divine messenger leading to trust
number 4: Dream materialization leading to courage
number 5: Transformation leading to personal freedom
number 6: Empathic abilities leading to healthy boundaries
number 7: Channeling higher wisdom leading to humility
number 8: Manifestation leading to personal integrity
number 9: Compassion leading to forgiveness
number 10: Leadership leading to perseverance
number 11: Illumination leading to spiritual awareness
number 12: Mastery leading to service and charity

Initiation Number 1: Interdependence
Leading to Honesty

The first thing I learned on my spiritual travels is that honesty without love leads to brutality. Welcoming the virtue of honesty into our lives is the practice of a deep soul cleansing and purification process. This virtue is a gift from living in a state of self-acceptance, love, and integrity in its highest form. It means respecting ourselves and making a commitment toward positive thinking.

When we adopt the understanding that we are not to be ashamed of what we think, say, feel, or do enough to lie about it, we develop an awareness that elevates the human consciousness. It consists of forming a bond of unconditional self-love free from judgment and limitations.

The benefits of honesty are endless, but the most obvious are lack of mental confusion, rise in self-esteem, throat and communication repair, cleansing the auric field, and a shift toward greater awareness. It is a pure state of mind and heart joined with the throat chakra.

Lies of omission can be worse than speaking an untruth. The harm falls within self-deception as well as the illusions being placed on another. Stop taking people hostage, and allow them the freedom to form their own thoughts with correct information.

We do not always tell ourselves the truth. Being honest with ourselves is another road to freedom. We discover our self-defeating tendencies by examining our self-talk. We realize ways we block ourselves from advancing toward our soul-life missions and make the necessary corrections to free ourselves.

A high level of attainment for the number 1 and the number 10 virtue is interdependence. This can be achieved only after learning the qualities of independence.

True independence is a choice of honoring our authentic selves above all masks of illusion and becoming clear conduits for divine Source to channel through us. It requires strength, innovation, creativity, and a fearless approach to demonstrate the unique qualities of thought, inspiration, imagination, and motivation.

Interdependence comes from the free will and balance of giving and receiving unconditionally to another person, place, or condition without fear of losing our identities as sovereign entities. It comes from personal integrity and self-attainment— of being strong and independent enough to acknowledge the value of sharing two whole structures in order to become more profitable.

Interdependence is moving from *me* to *we*.

If you have a 1 or a 10 in your chart, this initiation might rise up before some of the other virtues. It will ring true for you and naturally pull you through the door of entrepreneurship, teacher, and leader.

Initiation Number 2: Absolving Judgment Leading to Acceptance

This is not the most favorable initiation on our list, but it is one of severe importance. It is especially crucial for those who have the master number 11/2 in their soul-life agreements. This is just one of many lessons we need to implement in our lives in order to access the power and magic of the elusive number 11.

Acceptance is the second gate into spiritual awareness. It comes from absolving judgment or ceasing to view the world in terms of polarities such as good and bad. Acceptance is found when we are aware of our circumstances and choose to be at peace, knowing that everything is perfect exactly the way that it is and at all times. We accept the things that we cannot change, change the things that we cannot accept, and acquire the wisdom to know the difference.

We are addicted to pleasure in part because we confuse pleasure with happiness. We would say that deep down all we want is to be happy, but we do not have a realistic understanding of what happiness really is. Happiness is closer to the experience of acceptance and contentment than it is to pleasure. True happiness exists as the spacious and compassionate heart's willingness to feel whatever is in the present moment.

Concentration is best used to see the impermanent, impersonal, and unsatisfactory nature of all phenomena. These three insights are the keys to acceptance. Those who accept the world for how it is, rather than constantly wishing for something else, are on the road to freedom.

Initiation Number 3: Divine Messenger Leading to Trust

The number 3 gate is trust. The essence of the number 3 is about vulnerability, innocence, and childlike wonder. With all these qualities intact, we remain open to receive the truth offered by the higher realms. This initiation asks us to go back to our childhood awareness and trust that all our needs, including physical, emotional, mental, social, creative, and spiritual, are being taken care of.

When we were children, an adult most likely took care of our needs, but now that we have matured, a new developed relationship with a higher force that oversees everything in the universe is required.

When we passed through the gates of acceptance, we learned to let go of the illusion of control. We come to understand that our power lies in letting go and creating the ability to accept or change ourselves.

Another important aspect of trust is in our intuition. We rely on and trust our five senses to deliver to us the information we need to make accurate decisions about what is happening in our physical surroundings. Developing and using our sixth sense of intuition is vital to merging through the gates of higher wisdom. Our intuition comes in many forms and can vary from one person to the next. Intuition manifests from a hunch, gut feeling, dream, vision, or psychic form of claircognizance or inner knowing. The more we trust it, the more developed it becomes. It is an essential virtue for entering the gates of the higher realms. Trust and you shall receive.

Initiation Number 4: Dream Materialization Leading to Courage

All initiations are acts of personal power—a willingness to go beyond what you think your limitations are or the ability to do something that frightens you.

Courage is the choice and willingness to confront agony, pain, danger, uncertainty, or intimidation. Physical courage is bravery in the face of physical pain, hardship, death, or threat of death, while moral courage is the ability to act rightly in the face of popular opposition, shame, scandal, or discouragement in our personal lives.

Courage is a personality trait.

Every great leader, saint, and person of inspirational interest walked through the gates of courage and, more often than not, risked a value of personal gain to rise above fear to deliver his or her message.

Courage requires stepping outside our comfort zones and trusting our intuition enough to take action against all odds.

People whom have demonstrated selfless acts of valor include Joan of Arc, Gandhi, Oprah, Saint Francis, Steve Jobs, Einstein, and so on. Courage does not have to look monumental to the outside world; it just needs to be present in our daily lives.

Not all acts of courage need an audience. There are the spiritual acts of bravery that we succumb to when nobody is looking. These are quiet moments in seclusion when we surrender to our own truths and commit to a level of consciousness beyond our previous comprehension. It usually involves the shedding of old skin, willingness to surrender old beliefs, fears of the unknown, and willingness to grow wings to become a butterfly—the kind of courage that a caterpillar requires in the chrysalis process. It is a sojourn journey.

Initiation Number 5: Transformation
Leading to Personal Freedom

Personal freedom is the price we pay for spiritual evolution and when we are free from the limitations of social bondage, religious dogmas, and confinement of hereditary beliefs that no longer serve us.

People who work directly with the frequency of the number 5 know how precious personal freedom is, and they understand that this virtue is the main contributor to their success in life, whether it is in finances, relationships, or occupations.

Liberation is for the asking because freedom is a choice and not everyone is comfortable with personal freedom. Even though we do not always like the realities of our life situations, they become familiar. We do not like the dissatisfaction, suffering, and difficulty of life and even wish life were different, but we are so comfortable in it all because it is all we've ever known. Sometimes we would rather stay with the familiar than face the unknown, even when what is familiar is our suffering.

We are so used to our confusion that when the choice for freedom comes, we think, *No way!* It's too hard—because the unknown is too scary, we go through our lives repeating patterns of thought and action even when they bring us pain.

The Wikipedia definition for *freedom* is "having the ability to act or change without constraint. A person has the freedom to do things that will not, in theory or in practice, be prevented by outside forces. It is associated with having free-will and being without undue or unjust constraints, or enslavement, and is an idea closely related to the concept of liberty."

If we have passed through the previous gates and now have earned a sense of personal power that reflects our spiritual commitment and dedication to go beyond the material world that exists in the third dimension, then we enter into the magical world (fourth dimension) and then the miraculous world (fifth dimension) to find a whole new playground to expand and explore in.

Here in the higher octaves of enlightenment, there is prevalent access to the spirit realm. It is easier to connect with elevated intelligence, and when we ask for assistance in our personal freedom, there is instantaneous deliverance. It is truly liberating to be physically alone but surrounded by pure love and light from the other side, guiding us like a North Star.

When we choose freedom, it stems out of our act of courage to step above and beyond our comfort zones and even meet our spirit guides with open arms. Personal freedom is the choice and permission we give ourselves to explore options. Spiritual freedom is the key to the gate of higher awareness if and when we are ready to evolve.

Initiation Number 6: Empathic Abilities
Leading to Healthy Boundaries

Number 6 is the most empathic frequency of the single-digit numbers, and it is the vibration of both human and universal love. With all the psychic abilities available to this magical power, it is extremely important to acquire boundaries. Personal boundaries help to define an individual by outlining likes and dislikes and setting the distances one allows others to approach. This includes physical, mental, psychological, and spiritual boundaries involving beliefs, emotions, intuitions, and self-esteem.

Personal boundaries operate in two directions, affecting both the incoming and outgoing interactions between people.

These boundaries are sometimes referred to as *protection and containment.*

The type of protection and containment of boundaries is achieved through the practice of light boundaries. We have to be careful not to isolate ourselves from the outside world out of fear of attracting influences not congruent with our own personal energies. We deserve to walk free lives and to use our healing powers whenever we are called to take action. Empaths have the ability to pick up on the feelings and thoughts of others. This experience is not always pleasant when the emotions and thoughts of others are clouded by confusion and unskillful actions. We also have the ability to attract positive influences as well.

Before I learned about light boundaries, I had become a recluse, opting out of social events because I could not control my abilities. I had a strong desire to help people, but I felt vulnerable and helpless. Applying the light-boundary technique allowed me the freedom to do both—protect and contain my energy.

Light boundaries can be established by bringing the light down through the crown chakra and filling our hearts. We then surround ourselves with light protection and send the light from our hearts out to others in a continuous flow. It takes vigilance and daily practice, but once established, it becomes a natural practice, like breathing air.

**Initiation Number 7: Channeling
Higher Wisdom Leading to Humility**

In truth, there must be an act of humility when accepting all the initiations leading us through the gates of spiritual awareness. Honesty, acceptance, trust, courage, freedom, and boundaries ask us to drop the defenses of our egos (lower selves) in order to achieve a higher standard of living.

The number 7 holds the secret sauce to spiritual awareness and higher wisdom by combining forces with nature and her powerful faithful elements. Nature's true force lies within the infinite wisdom of a Higher Source. To become one with this altruistic magic, we must surrender our lower selves for a greater purpose.

Our egos are not bad. They were designed to protect us, but when we allow them to run our lives through fear, pride, vanity, greed, selfishness, and control, we disconnect from our ability to achieve greatness.

A spiritual journey will ask that we believe in a force more powerful than ourselves. Whether we choose to call it God, Universe, Nature, or Great Spirit, it is the ultimate surrender and infinite transformation to a higher way of being. Spiritual humility asks us not to lower ourselves to any person, place, or thing but rather to join forces with a greater power to achieve a higher standard of living.

When we find this calling or reach out for this initiation, we see that releasing the ego comes naturally because the price of keeping it is too high. When we join forces with this supreme intelligence, we become willing to surrender our pain for joy.

Initiation Number 8: Manifestation
Leading to Personal Integrity

Eights attract resources, and when connected to Higher Source, they create with the strength of an electric current similar to a steel rod in a lightning storm. Because of these extreme qualities, it is paramount that we learn and practice personal integrity.

By accepting and implementing the previous initiations into our lives, we begin to live in a state of grace. When we begin raising our awareness, we notice when anything or anyone around us is vibrating at a lower frequency, and our tolerance for this acceptance becomes weaker. We start attracting people of a higher caliber and make daily conscious choices to maintain quality vibrational circumstances in our lives.

This means having to weed out situations and people that no longer serve our greater good. This is one of the hardest things I have had to do, and it appears to be difficult for everyone I work with. It is called a *healthy selfishness.* This type of self-care is crucial when determining the quality of life we intend to live. We simply cannot walk two roads without consequences, and at some point, we will have to choose between the past and the present.

Personal integrity also means adopting communication skills that lead us to a higher state of being. Tools to grow in our awareness are available through many resources. The best guide that I have found and still use are the four agreements by Don Miguel Ruiz:

1. Be impeccable with your word.
2. Do not take things personally.
3. Do not make assumptions.
4. Always do your best.

These agreements changed my life. Maintaining personal integrity takes daily vigilance and commitment. The magic and power of this initiation is that when implemented in our daily lives, it has the ability to attract resources. It falls under the law of attraction. Like attracts like, and the higher we strive for personal integrity, we are assured greater possibilities that we create and integrate into our lives. It is one of the many rewards we receive through right living.

Initiation Number 9: Compassion
Leading to Forgiveness

This ninth initiation or virtue is about forgiveness and compassion. This is not only one of the most important keys but also a difficult key to access unless we are ready to open our hearts and discharge disappointments from the past.

If we have already adopted the previous initiations into our lives, they assist in preventing further situations or events from occurring that cause us to accumulate ongoing upsets that lead to disappointments and resentments.

The number 9 in numerology is about completion. What people do not often realize is that some strategies in life will eventually require closure, and often this won't happen unless a state of forgiveness is achieved.

When people choose to skip this initiation because they have entered the road of the unforgivable, they ultimately delay their ascent into the higher realms. Keep in mind that I come from my own experience and do not have access to everyone's particular circumstances. So, forgive me if what I am about to say appears insensitive. There are three types of forgiveness:

1. Forgiveness of others
2. Forgiveness of self
3. Forgiveness of the unforgivable

Forgiving others can best be seen under the light that we are all reflections of one another, meaning that when we point a finger at someone, we have three fingers pointing back at ourselves.

Oftentimes, the things we do not like in others are the things we refuse to acknowledge in ourselves. We attract people, places, events, and circumstances to reflect back to us what and where we need to grow. Relationships are called *the great mirrors* because they reflect back to our souls what we are truly feeling about ourselves. The feelings our souls have for others are indications of the sentiments, values, and worth our souls have for themselves. Our souls see themselves in the eyes of our brothers and sisters and realize what they need to do to heal. How our souls respond to others are indications of what the souls feel about themselves. This is a big truth to swallow, I know, but these initiations are keys to spiritual growth, and that requires that we be honest, courageous, and willing to develop insight where there was none before.

The second type of forgiveness is forgiving ourselves. After forgiving others by identifying ourselves in the mirror, discovering our imperfections in others, we forgive ourselves and direct compassion inward. We realize that we simply cannot give something that we do not have. When we acquire forgiveness and compassion toward ourselves, we extend it out to others, completely and without conditions.

The third type of forgiveness, or forgiving the unforgivable, is a little different. This falls under the unexplainable events or circumstances in our lives that we will not or cannot see our part in, including infidelity, drunk-driving fatalities, sexual assaults, cancer, terrorism, and so forth.

This is where other people fall off their divine paths and make choices that impact our lives in a negative way. Everyone has a divine path, and everyone has free will. Every challenge is an opportunity for growth, and often, these unforgivable circumstances that come into our lives occur to teach us forgiveness and compassion beyond the normal human experience.

If we allow it to be so.

This is one of the main initiations that I often work on with individuals in my program. We go into further depth to clear past disappointments, regrets, and resentments. It can be difficult to do this process alone.

Initiation Number 10: Leadership
Leading to Perseverance

A virtue is a moral excellence, and hope, faith, and love are the pillars that support the spiritual foundation from which all our dreams and desires take form. Without these three qualities, not much can weather the storms of time.

Hope is the seed, faith is the water, and love is the patience required to anchor this initiation in our lives. Hope is the ability to see greatness in the simple things. Faith is taking the action to secure the outcome. Love is the nurturing and harvesting to share with others.

The spiritual path can sometimes be a lonely journey unless we have found our tribe and become active in supporting our unique abilities and gifts. The number 10 is representative not only of individuality, creativity, and intuition but also of leadership.

The 0 in the equation gives it an extra boost of self-expression, sensitivity, and strength. This virtue of leadership and perseverance asks us to step out of our comfort zones and teach the world what we find to be true in our hearts. It requires faith in our abilities, connection to a Higher Source, and allows us to go beyond our conception of what we have already accomplished, creating a reality from tapping into our wildest dreams. Hope is the certainty that comes with the alignment of pure intentions—the knowledge that what we think, say, and do are for the betterment of all involved—and love is the fuel that sets everything in motion.

A high level of attainment for the number 10 virtue is interdependence. This can be achieved only after learning the qualities of independence. True independence is a choice of honoring our authentic selves above all masks of illusion and becoming clear conduits for divine Source to channel through us. It requires strength, innovation, creativity, and a fearless approach to demonstrate the unique qualities of thought, inspiration, imagination, and motivation.

Our needs within the relationship status have changed over time. The roles men and women have played within the romance and family dynamics have evolved.

We are merging out of two independent people living separate lives together into two independent people sharing their souls life path, purpose, and destinies. This is what is called "Interdependence".

A successful relationship is not when two independent people succeed to live parallel lives, it is when two people succeed to merge into one life willingly and support each other's growth emotionally, intellectually, and spiritually.

What is happening is the new relationship requirements are evolving into two whole people coming together and choosing each other because they want to and not because they need to.

This means that they want to share their gifts, abilities, and talents with each other in order to support their souls path and build on a common purpose that helps humanity evolve.

Interdependence is when two whole independent people complement each other and when they are together, their wholeness doubles the outcome of any endeavor and they find that they are much more esteemed together than apart.

We all yearn to be part of something beyond ourselves. We know in the depths of our soul that we are part of a greater connection and it is by merging our life with others to form a new life on a higher level that we find our true purpose and give our independence interdependent significance.

Interdependence is when people choose to need each other. They decide, based on their will and highest intention and not on their fears or weakness, to merge their lives. They choose to create a unified alliance out of recognition that it is more valuable than a life lived independently. An interdependent couple, friend or family member does not need each other, they want to be in each other's orbit. They understand that *we* is superior to *me*.

If you have a number 1 or 10 in your chart, this initiation might rise up for you before some of the other virtues. It will ring true for you and naturally pull you through the door of entrepreneurship, teacher, and leader.

Initiation Number 11: Illumination
Leading to Spiritual Awareness

The number 11 is a master number, allowing the two 1's to represent intuition and illumination. When both 1's are elevated and acting in alignment with a higher force, they equal Manifestation.

This is a natural portal to the higher realms, and by accepting the invitation to enter through the gates of spiritual awareness, we realize that this path is not always easy. Oftentimes, we get here by experiencing a life trauma or undergoing the dark night of the soul.

> Make no mistake about it—enlightenment is a destructive process. It has nothing to do with becoming better or being happier. Enlightenment is the crumbling away of untruth. It is seeing through the facade of pretense. It's the complete eradication of everything we imagined to be true. (Adyashanti)

Spiritual awakening or enlightenment entails being awake to our true nature, and it is no walk in the park, because to be aware of our true nature means we need to let go of all the false identifications and limited beliefs we have. This process in the spiritual awakening journey is referred to as the *dark night or spiritual death*. It is not death in terms of physicality but death of the false identifications we have with our egos, minds, and bodies.

When we begin to awaken to our infinite nature, our ego selves face a threat of death crisis and try to do everything in their power to maintain the status quo. When we begin to move forward on this awakening journey and embrace our true nature of being infinite and eternal beings, our egos give in and learn to collaborate with our souls.

Ego death is a kind of rite of passage wherein we realize that we are the infinite souls and egos are just the instruments we use, and this becomes the moment of our spiritual rebirth, when we step into our infinite nature and create our realities from a place of love and compassion. If we are going through the dark night of the soul, soon we realize our infinite nature and the cosmic miracle that we truly are! "The phoenix must burn to emerge."

When we accept spiritual awareness as an initiation and a virtue, it becomes a way of life, commitment, and dedication to live with open eyes, ears, heart, and speech. It is an inward and onward journey through enlightenment by being and staying in alignment with our soul-life agreements, which, in Egyptian numerology, are our sacred treaties and the reasons for being incarnated on this planet at this time.

Initiation Number 12: Mastery
Leading to Service and Charity

The number 12 in Egyptian numerology is the number of the master. This initiation is not specifically assigned to a single life-path number but instead is a universal initiation for all life paths.

It is a cycle number and a portal of transportation to the higher realms. It has great significance in our world. There are twelve months, hours on a clock, and disciples of Jesus, planets, astrological signs, and personality archetypes.

By accepting the key and entering this gate, we agree to walk a path of self-mastery. There are at least four common components or attributes that are acquired when we reach this gate: (1) elevated intuition, (2) psychic awareness, (3) contact with the spirit realm, and (4) selfless service to others.

The type of service offered to others with this initiation is not the kind for which we receive a reward or an exchange of money. We can by all means set up a business of service that requires an energy exchange of money, and there is nothing wrong with that, but with this particular initiation, it is the service we give to our communities or countries without conditions.

It does not have to require a lot of our time—a couple of hours a week, one day a month, or some such. The blessing of this virtue is that once we arrive here, it becomes a natural desire and not a chore to give freely of ourselves and our services.

A True Master Is the Artist and Leader of Humankind

The frequency of the number 12 belongs to souls who have walked the path of self-mastery. We think of Buddha, Gandhi, Jesus, Joan of Arc, and so forth, but there are many who have passed through this gate who are not famous. I call them human angels.

These are people who donate their lives to be of service to others or to make this world a better place without personal gain. We all have met people like this or at least know of someone like this. Even if we personally have not honed our gifts enough to bring them out to the public, we can always jump onto the wagon of somebody we admire who is offering a service of great value and help that person make a difference in the world until we are ready to birth our own gifts. Or, better yet, we can start our own causes for the betterment of our communities or the world in general. Here are some suggestions:

1. Finding alternatives to using plastic
2. Protecting our animals and environment
3. Helping the less fortunate

The wonderful thing about this initiation is that we will intuitively be called to take the action that is perfect for us. If we have had a calling for a long time, then this initiation is saying that it is *now* the time to take action.

<u>CHAPTER 4</u>

Journey of the Wounded Healer

When you honor your most authentic self—your Spirit—you are allowing your light to shine and touch the world. Living authentically, in its simplest terms, is living in your truth, the truth in your heart and soul. It is allowing yourself to be guided by Divine Truth and Wisdom, each and every day, and doing your Highest, most authentic work in the world. It is joyfully creating and living your Highest Purpose.

—*Valerie Rickel*

All messages from the great masters speak of the importance of fulfilling our purpose and soul-life missions. For those of us who incarnated with a high purpose to shift humanity into the light, the path has been lonely, disrupted, and not always clear.

I am called to share with you parts of my journey, especially those areas that are commonly difficult for people with high callings, and how I managed to overcome and dissolve the darkness, moving closer into the light.

I have several wounded-healer number frequencies in my birth and name chart. Understanding the powerful forces within their meaning and the prophecy behind their origin allows me to navigate the lessons and blessings I have chosen to experience in my lifetime.

Those of us who hold the responsibility of wounded-healer energy are not the same as those of other single-digit numbers. As much as we desire to blend into the norms of society, we always feel different and know deep down in our souls that there is more to life than eating, sleeping, working, and playing.

We are often called light workers, light warriors, star seeds, old souls, human angels, protectors of the earth, defenders of the light, speakers of the truth, guardians of the animals, worshippers of the moon, followers of the sun, seekers of enlightenment, believers in equality, and voices for victims.

This is a safe place for us to clearly recognize our purpose and origin. I encourage you to express your divinity by closing your eyes, putting your hand over your heart, breathing in the light, and exhaling the truth.

I started to express my unique characteristics at a young age. I will share my story with you.

"Fuel Your Passion and Follow Your Purpose ...

I have never been one who cared much about what people thought of me. When I was growing up, this attitude of mine worried my parents because it often led me into trouble.

I was an original thinker far beyond my years and spent a lot of time feeling like I did not belong in this world.

When I was in high school, I was bored, and the classes that interested me were not available. I decided not to waste my time and figured I really did not need a diploma to survive and succeed in life, so I chose to drop out of school.

Now, the principal had other plans for me. He called my father into the office, and all three of us gathered to discuss my future. They asked me what I wanted to do in order to complete my high school credits.

I told them the truth. I really wanted to go hiking in the backcountry for three months by myself, writing, drawing, and painting the wildlife that inspired me.

At that moment, the principal and my father made a secret pact to allow me to follow my passion, and one week later, I was dropped off in the mountains with supplies, harmonica, and my dog, Bruce.

I was sixteen years old at the time and feared society more than the lions, tigers, and bears I could have possibly encountered on my travels in the backcountry.

I have an 11/2 soul-life path number, and this requires that we have the courage to follow our passions or risk slow deaths of depression. I learned that when we stop at nothing to fulfill our dreams, the universe complies in mysterious ways.

On this journey, I wrote poems and songs and drew pictures of wildlife using plants to color my images. Even though there were moments I was afraid, especially at night, I was determined to conquer my fears to succeed in following my passion.

And yes, I graduated from high school knowing that when I lead with passion, against all odds, the universe opens doors even through the darkest of clouds."

My first book made many references to the master numbers, wounded healers, and the dark night of the soul. I want to explain exactly what a wounded healer is and the importance it plays in the role of master numbers. Besides it being a factor in master numbers, we also find these terms illustrated in the numerology of the number 6 and the number 9.

The definition essentially means that healers are spiritual warriors who have initiated the courage to vanquish the darkness of their souls, redeemed with wisdom and strength that create a light shining bright enough to guide, encourage, and inspire others to climb out of the shadows as well.

Depending on your numerology, the role of a wounded healer plays out for different reasons. I will break down and explain each number because they all have different reasons for incarnating under extreme circumstances, and they deserve accurate, proper attention because they all lead back to the importance of liberation for one and all of us.

I believe that before we are born, we sign up for our life events and experiences, especially those circumstances that are life altering, but I do not believe that we signed up to be victims or perpetrators, or that pain and abuse are even viewed and regarded the same in the spirit realm as they are after we incarnate in the third-dimension reality. I do believe that when we set up our soul-life agreements in the spirit realm, we understood our contracts through the eyes of karma, victory, and liberation, perceiving these occurrences as hopeful opportunities for growth, with the help of our spirit guides. It is the victory over these circumstances that we focused on before we came into this world and the hope of achieving the greatest-possible outcome. From this standpoint, we regarded our challenges as lessons and blessings instead of curses or punishments.

All experiences are necessary. When we view our lives with self-love and determine our experiences past or present not as good or bad but rather as necessary stepping-stones to our greater awareness and awakening, we move closer to fulfilling our life purpose.

I affirm that we willingly contracted for the experience but not the pain and suffering. Even though pain is part of the third-dimensional experience, we are meant to feel the pain, absorb the lesson, and move through it quickly, keeping in mind that feeling pain is inevitable, but suffering is optional. Walking through pain opens doors of least resistance. The less we resist, the clearer our paths become. If when experiencing pain, we ask, "What am I resisting?" and honestly seek the truth, we get a clear answer. If it is the truth that we are neglecting, then we ask our higher selves to show us the truth and ask Source to give us the courage to accept it. I have a prayer that I use:

> Source, be with me as I seek divine truth, reveal to
> me the light that aids me to see, give me the courage
> to do your will, and the strength and power to take
> action.

As we dive deeper to rediscover ourselves, we experience periods of time called the *dark night of the soul*. This is when we go through a difficult and significant transition, taking us into a deeper understanding of life and ourselves. We emerge from these shadow times like a lotus rising out of the mud, with a deeper level of clarity about who we are and what our true purpose is in life.

<u>CHAPTER 5</u>

Dark Night of the Soul

The universe not only gives us what we want; it gives us what we need. It uses any means possible to get our attention, including sickness, death, grief, loss, fear, and, in some circumstances, even the people we love. It discovers ways to show us what we have hidden in the depths of our being so we come back into remembrance, knowingness, and action. It delivers our conscious awareness back to the surface to address, heal, and learn everything that will lead us to our intended destinies.

I had power and light within me that frightened people, and many fought to extinguish me. I was a candle, young, inexperienced, and unaware of the power and light within. Being a child, I was naive and vulnerable to the forces of the wind, and my flame blew in countless directions.

At the time, I did not understand that when people feel threatened, they destroy the things they do not understand. All my life, I believed there was something wrong with me and was afraid to let my light shine. Thinking I was not good enough and something was wrong with me made me want to disappear—not want to be seen—and I tried to hide. Eventually allowing the turbulent winds of life to smolder the power and light burning within me, I lodged the remaining flicker deep down in the burrows of my soul until darkness overtook my path and I stumbled trying to find my way.

To heal, I had to find the original incident in my life that had caused my initial descent into darkness and pain. Once I identified it, I located the pattern that had allowed my light to be extinguished. This wound needed to be healed at the very site where it originated. I did not need to dwell there; I just needed to feel the feeling and create a different outcome. Once relit, I became a torch, an unrelentless passion of healing joy.

I'd once heard that if we hold on to a feeling for more than fifteen seconds, it is because we enjoy it or it is serving us on some level. In order to change a painful memory, I had to find the feeling, belief, or memory that I wanted to change, experience it in my body in its entirety, and then switch it to a better and different outcome or vision and hold this better feeling for seventeen seconds. I repeated this exercise several times until it transmuted the old belief into my new memory and reality.

As healers, we need to heal ourselves. We may become too busy healing other people and do not take the time to heal ourselves. We get distracted in the process of having to put everyone else's healing crisis first and then become shocked when we find ourselves in the midst of our own crises. What happens quite often is we ignore our own emotional hiccups until they become blaring illnesses demanding immediate attention. I started to become aware that I was attracting people who needed healing exactly in the areas where I was working on myself. Coincidence? I think not.

We must go into the dark night of the soul and make peace in this darkness by being brave and lighting a candle. We become torches in a world filled with fear and negativity. In theory, when lighting our torches, the darkness slips away, or everything that was in the dark becomes illuminated. We cannot be afraid to own our truth and be the light we are meant to live. We will not be able to help others heal if we are not willing to heal ourselves.

May Your Heart Beat to the Brightened Path of the Golden Sun

The truth is that although we are all born with souls, not all of us know how to fully embody and integrate them into our human experience. In our modern world, we get pulled to live egocentrically rather than soul-centrically. Mystics, saints, and shamans throughout history have referred to this egocentric human struggle in different ways. But the one thing they all have in common is their pointing to the need for us to consciously grow into our divine potential.

These days, the concept of the dark night of the soul is used in a much broader sense. What was once a term reserved for people actively going through a spiritual journey has now become the label for anything ranging from a few bad days to a mild depression.

Traditionally, the *dark night of the soul* refers to the experience of losing touch with our God or Creator and being plunged into the abyss of godless emptiness. The modern understanding of having a dark night of the soul is not exclusively a religious one. It often means losing all meaning in life, feeling out of touch with the divine, feeling betrayed or forsaken by life, and having no solid or stable ground to stand on.

What Is the Dark Night of the Soul?

It is a period of spiritual desolation, disconnection, and emptiness in which one feels totally separated from the divine. Those who experience the dark night feel completely lost, hopeless, and consumed with anguish. It is similar to severe spiritual despondency.

This concept has existed for a long time and spans back to the sixteenth century, when poet and Catholic mystic Saint John of the Cross wrote a poem titled "La noche oscura del alma (the Dark Night of the Soul)." Saint John wrote, "If a man wishes to be sure of the road he's traveling on, then he must close his eyes and travel in the dark."

The dark night of the soul is not just depression, because depression has its roots in biological chemical imbalances and unhealthy thought patterns and surfaces from personal loss, mental illness, physical illness, abuse, and genetics.

It is a different experience because it is primarily a spiritual form of crisis that cannot be treated or cured with therapy or psychiatry. Those of us going through the dark night feel an increasing sense of hopelessness, unease, and despair when we discover that no one can save us but ourselves. Inevitably, we feel more alone, frustrated, and confused about the world and ourselves.

When depression ends, very little changes in our lives in terms of beliefs, values, and habits, but when the dark night ends, everything in our lives is transformed and enhanced with an astonishing view through the looking glass of new eyes.

Polish psychologist Kazimierz Dabrowski once coined a term called *positive disintegration*, viewing tension and anxiety as necessary in the process of spiritual and psychological maturation, "It is the friction within us causing the mirror of our souls to be polished clear enough to glimpse our true nature."

A true dark night of the soul leaves a long-lasting impact because it changes us completely. When exiting a dark night, we discover that something is always taken away from us (for the better), such as our beliefs, perceptions, former meaning in life, or even our egos.

The metaphysician Ananda Coomaraswamy put it this way: "No creature can attain a higher grade of nature without ceasing to exist."

When a butterfly begins to emerge from its cocoon, it must struggle to strengthen its wings, and if someone frees the butterfly from its cocoon prematurely, it will not fly because its crucial tempering stage has not occurred.

The same is true for trees. Trees need wind to build their structural strength to stay upright, and our dark night of the soul is our wind, our cocoon; it is an ego death whereby we shed the egos preventing us from embodying our souls.

If we avoid the hard work of, as Ananda put it, "ceasing to exist," or breaking down our old confining structures, we deny our ability to truly embody our essential nature.

It is terrifying when the ground beneath our feet is ripped out from beneath us, and this is precisely what we experience during this process.

Before any true growth or healing occurs, there must be a development of destruction and complete annihilation of everything we thought would bring us happiness.

There are three ways that spiritual awakenings occur: (1) at the hands of wise spiritual teachers, (2) through the spiritual motivation of soulfully mature people, and (3) spontaneously because of life circumstances.

Spontaneous awakenings arrive in several ways: We experience changes in intensely uncomfortable ways. We may lose our jobs, get betrayed by our romantic partners, lose people close to us, receive terminal diagnoses, face near-death experiences, be involved in physical accidents, experience suicidal depression, contend with the destruction of our homes or homelands, or lose our religious faith. Why do these things happen to us? Because we are meant for so much *more* than what we have. When the universe intervenes, it is because we did not have the courage to seek it out unless we were put in a severely difficult position. If you find yourself in this situation, always ask to be shown the best possible outcome for everyone involved because the biggest blessings are disguised as the lowest points in our lives.

The dark night is an omen of change that lets us know we cannot continue living the way we have been living. There is no growth and no awakening without our first seeing and acknowledging our existing disappointments.

Acknowledging our disappointments means becoming aware of a deeply held sense of incompletion that we all carry within us. It means becoming aware that something is desperately missing from our lives, and those who have experienced or are currently experiencing a dark night of the soul know that something fundamental at a core level is out of focus or balance or completely lacking in their lives—and that so much more is possible in their lives even though they do not know exactly what it is.

The solution to or freedom from our suffering and disconnection from the divine realm is through methods of purging, cutting away, dislodging, disintegrating, and clearing old pieces of our lives so that we can begin afresh.

The dark night is a process of shedding our old homes and going in search of new ones. This process requires a huge leap of faith into the abyss of the unknown, which comes at quite an abrupt and frightening pace.

If you think you are going through this journey, it is important that you understand that many of us have been where you are, and many people still are. There is no map or GPS; there is only the flickering luminescence of your soul to light the way.

I hope our work encourages, empowers, and supports you while you undertake the descent into your underworld. You are never alone, and soon that small flicker within will become a guiding torch for the next person receiving this lesson and blessing.

CHAPTER 6

Decoding the Numerology of the Wounded Healer

In numerology, the master number 11 symbolizes an activation code, an awakening, and a message from the higher realms. The number 1 is similar to the letter I and represents intuition, illumination, intelligence, and inspiration. Those of us magnetized by this energy answer a higher calling by tuning in to the voice of Spirit.

When 11 appears in our numerology charts, it indicates we were born with a spiritual calling, to walk a path of authenticity, and to help others. The 11 is auspicious and does not follow the same guidelines as other numbers. Those of us who carry the influence of the master number 11 are meant to break rules, open doors, free the soul and most importantly, master our lives. All master numbers use master number 11 as their base code of ethics because all master numbers are a multiple of 11.

The number 1 relates to creativity, strength, intelligence, and independence and is a conduit from matter to Spirit. We can easily see this demonstration in the form of a straight line. When the 1 is doubled, the energy and momentum are intensified, allowing portals to open in the form of an awakening.

People with 11 energy will be given the opportunity in their lifetimes to achieve a spiritual awakening, and because we all have free will, some may choose to keep these doors closed. The problem is that not moving forward will cause anguish in some areas of our lives.

This is why I wrote this book—to encourage all warriors of the light to answer their calling, because when the pain of avoidance is greater than the fear of becoming, the shift occurs.

{Note that if you have a master number above the 11/2, you should refer to the properties of the 11/2 in addition to the master number you are seeking. It is important to understand the frequencies of the master number 11/2 because all master numbers carry this quality as their base structure. You can find the meaning behind specific master numbers (11–99) in my book *Egyptian Numerology: Emergence into the Fifth Dimension.*}

Those of us carrying these powerful forces do not fully mature into our energy until the age of forty or older. Until then, we are working through the lessons of the lower number in the equation. These lessons are a prerequisite, necessary to fully establish the enormous power offered by the higher number. If the lessons are not learned before the master number activates, there are always difficulties and challenges in handling the energy. The universe will thrust us into circumstances demanding that we grow. We set up timelines, cycles, people, places, and events to occur in order to keep us aligned with our mission and our purpose, and those of us who chose to be wounded healers will intuitively know that we are here to do big things.

Master Number 11/2: Wounded Healer—The Prophet

The wounded healer of this master number is more karmic than single-digit numbers. These wounded healers come into this lifetime specifically to work off past karma. They must transcend more difficulties to excel in life. Many are original thinkers, end up working alone, or find themselves in a position to defend their ideas against a hostile majority. They may choose physical disabilities, mental afflictions, or abusive and painful childhoods to work through in this incarnation. Their complicated lifestyles lead them to be viewed as outsiders or outcasts or completely insane. Frequently, they isolate from ordinary society because they feel so misunderstood and do not have a desire to lead normal lives. In some cases, they end up fighting against the tide their entire lives because they view trying to fit into a world they do not understand as being too painful. It can take a long time for a master number to be accepted by other people, so many of them are late bloomers.

The 11/2 is the number for bisexuality, homosexuality, and transgenderism because of the duality aspects of the number 2. These wounded healers tend to live lives of extremes, and in their quest to find a balance between the rational and irrational, male and female, they will pursue the most eclectic of religions, cultures, and pursuits. Statistically, a small percentage of people are born with number 11 in their birth charts, yet they gravitate and congregate in areas where spiritual awareness is encouraged. When out of balance and working out of their lowest-energy vibration, they can be self-centered, insecure, codependent, reclusive, and depressive and express various addictive tendencies.

Their lessons are meant to teach them to open up their deeper sensitivities and empathic abilities. Trusting and strengthening their highly developed intuition brings them closer to nature, angels, spirit guides, and opens their awareness to the outer realms, such as animals and the elemental kingdom.

They are here to listen to their inner voices and channel higher wisdom. Although many 11s have tough and incredibly challenging lives with little to encourage a spiritual path, they ultimately find the tenacity and extraordinary strength to match all the challenges they have incurred. These avant-garde and visionary individuals make great students, psychics, mystics, healers, teachers, writers, musicians, and artists. They have outstanding channeling, psychic abilities, and a special connection with a Higher Source, allowing wisdom to pour directly through them.

The number 11 represents two pillars—a gateway opening a direct portal between (1) inspiration and (2) illumination. When these two pillars are activated, it creates a momentum for manifestation. When examining the number 1, we notice it is the only number that is completely straight up and down, like a column or antenna. The number 1 is an unobstructed channel of energy or direct conduit between the spiritual and physical worlds. It is the number of initiations, invention, and new beginnings that flow to us in the form of ideas and inspiration. When this number is doubled, the energy becomes exponentially powerful and is the master number of creation, expression, and manifestation.

11:11 is a powerful portal for manifestation. 11:11 adds up to the number 4 (1+1+1+1=4). The number 4 represents the elements, Earth, matter, and physical manifestation. It is an indication that we co-create with Source, and we have the power to manifest (4) whatever we are inspired to create (1). The master number 11 teaches us how to be a master manifestor.

The lower number (2) of a master number combination is a prerequisite for the power of the higher frequency (11). It is important to understand that simply having a master number in one's birth chart does not qualify anyone as having something of significance. It is merely an opportunity for one to choose a door to enter through and a frequency to master.

The number 2 in this combination is a doorway that leads to the magic frequency of the 11. When speaking of energy, I mention the duality concept involved, especially when the number 2 appears in the sequence. There are high and low vibrations available to us with any number. Acquiring access to the energy of the higher frequencies of a number will always depend on how evolved we are on the spiritual realm. Keeping in mind that we attract the same vibration that we exist on at any given moment. I include ways to heighten our vibration and encourage everyone on the 11 path to raise their energy field.

Let us look at the number 2 and how evolving spiritually prepares us for the magic available through the master number 11. In the roman numeral II, this number appears as two 1's standing side by side and so is the symbol of the number 11. The number 2 resonates with balance, peace, beauty, justice, creativity, and the union of two equal 1's coming together to form a relationship. These are natural number 2 properties and tendencies. To get a better idea of the qualities needed to advance into the number 11, refer to the initiation and virtue of the number 2 in chapter 3, "Becoming the Miraculous Healer."

When people with the number 2 vibrate at a lower frequency, they become out of balance, and they struggle, often experiencing codependency, addiction, disharmony (complaining), insecurity, frequent self-doubt, lack of motivation, procrastination, and mild to severe depression.

They also tend to overeat and be addicted to sugar (craving sweetness in their lives)

Master Number 22/4: Wounded Healer—The Manifestor

Building castles in the air and pulling them down to manifest expression here on earth is a gift bestowed on master number 22. "Building castles in the air" is a phrase used to illustrate the acute use of imagination that those of this number have available to them. It comes from the number 11 doubled, allowing for strong intuition, inspiration, imagination, illumination, and awareness. The 22 is known as the master manifestor.

These wounded healers have all the abilities of the master number 11 available, as well as the gift of manifestation. Their path is to stay focused, learn to channel higher wisdom, and build the grandest castle that serves the greater good.

The master number 22 contains the superpower of dream materialization with incredible perception and intuition—access to a dream or vision world and the ability to ground it down into reality through a system of rounded, tangible effort, work, and action. These individuals get intuitive insights guiding them like the North Star in the physical world. They can be dream-materialization architects by taking their vision and solidifying it in the physical world so everyone can enjoy a new foundation and way of experiencing life.

They uniquely create their own realities and must follow their North Star and dare to be different. They are the trailblazers, trendsetters, and master cultivators who possess certain gifts, strengths, and weaknesses that others do not. They have extra protection from the angels and a green light to manifest! Whatever those of this number think about is sure to become a reality; therefore, it is exceedingly important they choose their thoughts carefully. If they are willing to work toward manifesting their desires, then enormous prestige, success, and fame can easily be achieved. They are endowed with many exceptional powers and a unique talent for manifesting ideas into the realm of reality. Sometimes they display what looks like insensitivity, but they are just extremely focused on their goals. Their spiritual directive is to be detached from their wealth and spread it among the masses to make others' lives easier.

One of the most confusing elements a 22/4 will encounter is by skipping the crucial lessons offered by the lower equation in the number 4. They can get lost in the quaking emergence that comes with this master number and become restless, reckless, and impatient while burning up a ton of energy, running in circles, and accomplishing nothing. This course of action leads to depression, senseless complaining and total burnout before they even get off the ground with their life purpose.

The number 4 energy is grounding, stable, methodical, and secure. If individuals have matured and aligned the 11 energy, the power of the 22/4 will automatically slide into place, giving them a sense of creativity and motivation to move forward with their goals in life.

The 22/4's are here to learn about the importance of family, roots, and stability. *Seeing one's future through the eyes of the past* refers perfectly to this master number. If there is anything blocking a passageway to the family, it is crucial 22/4's work through these circumstances and not run from them. Family lessons help them escalate the spiritual-growth process and quite possibly lead toward their life purpose.

Here's to the crazy ones, the misfits, the rebels, the troublemakers, the round pegs in the square holes. The ones who see things differently— they are not fond of rules—you can quote them, disagree with them, glorify or vilify them, but the only thing you can't do is ignore them because they change things. They push the human race forward, and while some may see them as the crazy ones, we see genius, because the ones, who are crazy enough to think that they can change the world, are the ones who do. (Steve Jobs)

If out of balance, the master number 22/4 may lean toward obsessive-compulsive disorders and become addicted to perfection. The number 4 comes here to work out health issues and to balance out past karma. They come in as wounded healers to learn compassion and empathy when assisting others to heal.

Number 6: Wounded Healers—The Light Keepers

Possessing empathy and having a heart connection to all things allow a person to be a direct channel for the healing grace of Source. These individuals' medicinal nature concedes them as the nurturers and caretakers for family, friends, and community. The number 6 is the vibration of love, both human and universal. It is the number of the wounded healer.

Egyptian numerology states that people who have this number in their birth charts were healers in a past life and met their untimely demise as a result of their healing abilities, therefore finding it hard to step up as healers in this life. They often have health issues that defy treatment, they struggle with health care remedies, never making a breakthrough until they stop and say, "Okay God, here I am," making a promise to be of service as a healer. They continue to search for healing answers empty-handed until they make a commitment to be of service. They make excellent counselors and need to go into the healing fields of body, mind, and soul—not just psychology but hands-on healing.

Those on the number 6 path are being asked to come back into their authentic path and be true to themselves in several avenues. This is influenced by Chiron, a comet that orbits the Sun, revealing their power to process trauma and suffering so that they can in turn heal others. Chiron represents the saying "Heal thyself" and points to the wounded healer.

These people love and believe the greatest expression of inner divinity is through teaching and guiding others. They are the happiest when seeing positive results of their influence blossom in other people. The number 6 has a truly outstanding sense of responsibility, love, and balance. They are helpful and ever conscientious, making them quite capable of rectifying and balancing any sort of inharmonious situation. They are inclined to give help and comfort to those in need. They have a natural penchant for working with the old, dying, sick, or underprivileged. Although they may have considerable creative and artistic talents, chances are that they will devote themselves to an occupation that shows concern for the betterment of the community. They have a strong drive to help others, and this trait is rooted in their high sensitivity and empathic nature. They are often found in career paths that enable them to use these qualities, such as teaching, therapy, nursing, and healing.

The most precious lesson for those on the number 6 path is learning how to heal themselves with the same love and compassion they give to others. They will be dealing with relationship issues in this life, and it is the relationships first with themselves, second with the source of their understanding, and thirdly with another person—in this order!

These people are often masked as light workers. A light worker is essentially a person, a soul who incarnates into physical form and is dedicated to shining light into the world. He or she anchors the higher dimensional light of Spirit and Divine into the physical realm to help others usher forth transformation on earth. They are here to bring earth out of darkness and into greater levels of light, connection, peace, harmony, and authenticity.

Light workers have a strong sense that they are different, and although they know they are a human being, they really do not belong here on earth. This manifests as a feeling of alienation, isolation, or even homesickness. They feel that they are on the outside looking in and can have a deep underlying feeling of wanting to go home.

Light workers are driven to understand the world better by seeking out extreme experiences. Many are wounded healers and have experienced the dark night of the soul at least once in their lifetimes. With these experiences comes great empathy, which causes them to feel what others feel very deeply. This gives them leverage to develop their healing abilities to fulfill their true purpose in their lifetimes.

They often do not fit into traditional authority models or modern workplace structures, and they do not feel comfortable in them. This is largely due to their antiauthoritarian nature. Internally, they have a strong resistance to anything that places value on the dark side of power or hierarchy, and this prompts a rebellious response from them.

Expression, beauty, and development are important to them, and they gravitate to energy outlets such as writing or the arts to release their creative nature and serve as a voice for humanity. It is common for them to be drawn into activities that nurture their spirituality, and this can be anything from meditating or spending time in nature to reading self-help books.

When light workers are enlightened and self-actualized, they recognize this drive as their true purpose in life and find their own fulfillment in guiding themselves and others toward spiritual insights.

Because they have acute empath abilities, I teach people under the influence of the number 6 to shield themselves with light boundaries (refer to chapter 14, "Protection"). There is a way for empathic people to learn how to shield their energy when in and around groups of people to elevate the energy in the room and express their true nature without soaking up any outside energy. They should never diminish their energy at any time, for anyone, or for any reason. They must be the light that they are and shine, shine, shine!

Number 9: Dark Night of the Soul—The Druid

From an early age, these people carry an eternal sense of justice for humanity and equality. They are considered old souls, described as wise beyond their years.

Egyptian numerology states that they came into this lifetime as wounded healers because in their past lives, they died helpless, hopeless, powerless, and enraged, and it bled over into the present life. They are now being asked to turn anger and hurt into love, compassion, and forgiveness in all situations and circumstances. It is their missions and purposes in this lifetime. They need to overcome their challenges, be of service in some big way to help humanity and make this world a better place.

Those on the number 9 path often face a unique challenge at some point in their lives that is a test of faith. Usually, this incident takes the form of a devastating personal loss, disease, or some sort of tragedy that triggers the dark night of the soul. It is during this period of their lives that they find the extreme courage and strength to become wounded healers.

These people acquire a spiritual development that accompanies situations that force them to let go of emotional issues and connections that interfere with their higher purpose and life mission.

When 9 appears in individuals' paths, they have come to earn a completion. This is why forgiveness, compassion, integrity, justice, higher wisdom, and selfless service have been important all their lives. These are tools necessary for their ascension to the next level of awareness. The number 9 is the warrior, white knight, walker of light, and integrity, and anyone who stands next to these individuals is protected and guaranteed integrity without judgment or fear.

Those on this path have a tendency to be reclusive or entertain a hermit lifestyle mainly because inherently they do not want to accumulate more drama or karma in this lifetime. Those who walk this path gift the world with sage wisdom and incredible kindness, reminding us that by allowing our own divine light to shine, we can change the world. This energy serves the greater good.

The number 9 symbolizes sanctuary, contemplation, and self- awareness. This true path of the seeker eventually leads to ascension. Spirituality cannot abide stagnant water, and these individuals have an unquenchable thirst and desire to understand the greater mysteries in life with natural tendencies to look within and above for all answers to the questions asked from the mundane world. They may even go to remote locations to search their souls in quest for the ultimate truth and will likely do this several times in their lives as necessary to process new information they have encountered and acquired.

They are rarely consumed with worldly ways, and nature is found as the ultimate teacher. This is true not just for pure solitude reasons but for the unlimited lessons the wilderness provides. The life path of the number 9 eventually leads to one of selfless service and the humanitarian way, using love and inspiration as a drive to solutions. Throughout their lives, in this incarnation, they illustrate their spiritual path through deeds more than words because they walk the talk, and honor is a solid virtue.

They are visionaries, healers, psychics, and artists as portrayed in the tarot of the hermit, depicting the 9 as a wise old man. One hand bears a lantern of sagacity lighting the way, the other a staff of authority to steady his feet. As he stands in the wastelands, he breathes a sigh; the burdens of the shaman, walker between worlds, lead to a life of reclusion. That moment of silence is one of prayer, when the hermit listens to the voice of the Divine and returns to the world with a message. These individuals are a channel to higher wisdom.

CHAPTER 7

You Cannot Heal the World Until You Heal Yourself

Physician, heal thyself
—Luke 4:23

Before we build a bridge from suffering to liberation, we must remove blatant obstacles from our paths. Overcoming adversities is the biggest lesson we face as wounded healers. The most common obstructions faced on our route to becoming miraculous healers are abandonment, rejection, betrayal, resentments, and judgments.

The next few chapters discuss dissolving the inner conflicts blocking our flow and keeping us handicapped, debilitated, and cemented in our darkness. Instead of fighting our inner demons, we examine them with curiosity, learning why they have come to reside. Offering them love and understanding each time they penetrate our lives grants us access to a new freedom and better way of living.

If we seek truth, we need to be prepared to investigate our darkness as well as the light within. If we seek to know ourselves, we need to be prepared to maintain the light when we see our darkness. The more cognizant we are that we create our realities, the less they need to fall apart to get our attention.

Liberation Is For the Asking

To walk an authentic path takes courage. Disengaging from conformity and fear is risking rejection. We choose this path, but in essence, it chooses us. We must look deeply into our truth and surrender to darkness and transformation, rebirthing ourselves out of the fires of our souls. Wisdom arises from the intermingling of knowledge and experience found in the magical cauldron of transformation, life's most precious gift to us, an offering that requires us to give our greatest gifts, talents, and abilities back to life and humanity.

Liberation is for the asking because freedom is a choice and not everyone is comfortable with personal freedom. Even though we do not always like the realities of our life situations, they become familiar. We do not like the dissatisfaction, suffering, and difficulty of life and even wish life were different, but we get comfortable in it all because it is all we have ever known. Sometimes we would rather stay with the familiar than face the unknown, even when what is familiar is our suffering.

When we become grounded in our confusion and the choice for freedom comes up, we think, *No way!* It's too hard—because the unknown appears too scary, we go through our lives repeating patterns of thoughts and actions even when they bring us pain.

It is my experience that not everyone wants liberation. People may romanticize the idea of personal liberation and freedom, but when it comes down to taking the necessary action, the fuel behind the engine dies down to a low hum and eventually fades to a whisper.

When we awaken to the realization that we are enslaved not only to our body but through the process of birth amnesia, we begin to arouse closer to our true souls' journey.

We ask ourselves, "What do I have to give up in the process of liberation?" and "How does imprisonment serve me?" The walls of a prison can become safe and familiar no matter how uncomfortable they are. There are always consequences when we choose to evolve, and unfortunately, before change can occur, the pain of staying stuck needs to become greater than the fear of leaving our confinement.

We are all born free in spirit but not necessarily in our circumstances. Our economic, genealogic, and environmental influences may very well dictate just how liberated we truly feel when we incarnate into this world. We have all been in situations or have known someone who has been tested in areas of mental sanity, emotional stability, and even physical abilities. It would not be a colorful life without our challenges and lessons to overcome, but the one thing we all have in common when we arrive on this planet is that we are liberated in spirit. This is one thing that no one can take from us, not even in death. So, it might be safe to say that everything beyond our spirits can be manipulated by circumstances in one way or another, and if this is true, then the only thing that is totally free is the soul. Everything else is subject to *illusion*. No one can take our love, light, power, dignity, or integrity unless we give it away. We can be treated with disrespect, deception, and abusive behavior, but no one can own or enslave our souls. Illusions are deceptive.

When I mention the word *illusion*, I am not referring to the validity of circumstances, because what we are experiencing in any given moment is our reality, but what I am saying is that it can be subject to change. Our realities can change if we change our perceptions and circumstances. I find that if I change my perception, my circumstances inevitably change.

It is safe to say that if I can change my perceptions, I can change my belief systems behind the object that I perceive. Sometimes I react without knowing what my belief systems are and how they got there. I have found that the only way I can change these things is if I am challenged and willing to explore their existence. The only way I can become willing is if I am uncomfortable and suffering, convinced that I can no longer move forward with the information I am working with, and the pain of staying stuck is greater than the fear of growing.

I treasure the saying "At the end of the day, the only questions I will ask myself are, Did I love enough? Did I laugh enough? Did I make an impact on the world?" What matters most at the end of our lives is how much we absolutely loved. Now, it is difficult for me to feel love when I am in crisis or experiencing fear, loss, frustration, or even confusion. It is even difficult for me to experience the sensation of love before I have my first cup of coffee in the morning!

This book's subtitle, *Liberation Is for the Asking*, derives from a dream that I had three months before the rug was pulled out from underneath me. It came to me like a warning—or was it a life raft? Looking back, I think it was little of both.

I uncovered information disclosing the fact that the man I loved and had been living with for several years was having an affair with another woman, who was a fellow healer belonging to our prayer circles, and this apparently had been going on for months. My initial reaction was like being hit in the stomach with a baseball bat and getting the wind knocked out of me. It felt like the life had been vacuumed right out of my body. Immediately, my hidden emotions of abandonment, rejection, and betrayal swept through my body like a wildfire. Out of control, untamed, and dangerous, I leaped into a state of PTSD that lasted for several months, and I fell into a dark abyss of emotional waters that continued to swell around me day after day.

For me, I have experienced many different types of betrayal, rejection, and abandonment, and the most damaging involves sexuality. We are the gatekeepers of our own sexuality. But when a lover, partner, spouse, friend with benefits, or intimate partner betrays our trust in a committed relationship, things can get emotionally messy fast.

I am stronger now because of this experience because instead of becoming a victim of betrayal, I got to see the gift in the betrayal that happened *for me* instead of *to me*. I found a bigger lesson here, and it had to do with all my past betrayals, abandonments, and rejections. This particular betrayal touched my present circumstances but also all the ones from childhood on up. Just to clarify, experiencing multiple betrayals does not mean that we are doormats. It does not mean that we are not worthy of love, but we have to be honest about our feelings and understand their hidden messages in order to move beyond suffering.

Unprocessed emotional traumas, especially sexual, create lifelong disease.

If we do not take action on the betrayals that have happened for us, we are literally killing ourselves because these emotions sit like sludge in our hearts, sacral, kidneys, lungs, and livers until they are cleared. We manifest autoimmune symptoms and permit a continued cycle of the same betrayals.

It keeps us in the loop of self-sabotage, and when we open up and find the first core betrayal in our sexuality, we are no longer hiding and blocking these emotions from our energy fields. Being bold and brave and addressing all our betrayals are part of the process of major transformation.

We can always run from toxic relationships, but if we do not heal what attracted the toxic people to us, we will meet them again. The same demon—just in a different person and circumstances. We stop repeating the cycle when we move on not only from the people who hurt us but from the versions of ourselves that gave people the power over us.

We were never created to live depressed, defeated, guilty, condemned, ashamed, or unworthy. We were created to be liberated!

Before I found liberation, I had to go through the grieving process as though one would with the death of a loved one: denial, anger, bargaining, depression, and acceptance. I had to grieve the loss of a relationship I thought I had, an illusion, a dream, and a mark in time that had once existed. Life as I knew it ended in an instant, and I was not prepared. I was blindsided, truly devastated, and in a bad place when the voice from my dream repeated itself: "liberation is for the asking." But what does that mean? I thought, *How do I find liberation from this dark, lonely, deep hole that I have dug myself into? How do I climb out of betrayal? How do I even begin?*

At that moment, I asked, prayed, begged, and even cried for liberation. I emptied out all my reserves for this single impossible request. I got up, dusted myself off, and waited for an answer. This led to my making an appointment with a local shaman who'd been suggested to me by a dear friend who'd had success with him after dealing with grief from the death of her husband. The shaman conducted a simple vision quest ceremony with me that consisted of his special abilities and my willingness to feel my pain and suffering.

What came to surface was my association with betrayal, rejection, and abandonment not only from this particular episode but from my childhood in this lifetime and from other lives. I was shown psychic and emotional doorways to pass through, as well as visions of my future self. This shamanic journey was deep and cleansing. I felt the earth move underneath my feet for several days afterward as my life adjusted itself with all this new information.

The most alarming discovery was just how comfortable I had become in the position of being the victim. I was ashamed of how familiar and comfortable it sat with me. My friends and family could identify with my situation, and I received a lot of attention and sympathy. Although this was gratifying on so many levels, it did not empower me. I kept saying to myself, "Where is the liberation in this?" There is absolutely nothing liberating about being hurt and angry. Nothing at all! The grieving process made sense to me, but when I got to the acceptance part, I had to ask myself, "What do I accept out of this situation that is going to make me feel at peace?" I could accept my reasons for being hurt and angry, and then the victim cycle would repeat itself. I needed to find a way out of this destructive loop. "OK, God, what is liberation?" The next week, I was in a healing group, and a friend gave me a psychic message. He told me that I needed to "break the mold."

I took this to mean that I need to go further and deeper spiritually than I had ever delved before. *Bingo.* When I imagined going beyond the mold of victimization, I was finally free from emotional and mental trauma. I was truly liberated, if only for a moment. Acceptance is not a state of being; it is a doorway to walk through leading to a new frontier.

Could it be that this whole set of dire circumstances had been set in motion only to lead me through this etheric doorway, showing me that there was more for me to discover, explore, and become? Why did I have to *become* in an enormous amount of pain before I was ready to be pushed to the inner limits of my belief system? How did I not recognize this doorway toward evolution within my hours of quiet meditation? I knew that I had to believe and imagine my life beyond pain before I could find the doorway, and most of all, I had to ask for liberation before I was willing to receive it.

The mold from which I needed to break free was a prison wall of pure resistance. It was my fear and illusion that kept me the victim of my circumstances because I had never risen above the consciousness of betrayal in this life or any other, apparently. In the past, whenever I would experience these feelings, I would turn to self-righteous anger and hold on to these experiences as they sank deep into my consciousness. I never processed these feelings; I distracted myself with whatever I could get my hands on because I believed the pain would eventually kill me. This is the behavior I'd been previously taught, and this process guaranteed and destined these dramas to continue to play repeatedly in my life until I was ready to change the pattern and break the mold.

First, I had to examine my pattern, which was to attract partners who displayed behaviors leading me to feel unimportant, invisible, and not good enough and to question the validity of my personal integrity.

In the past, I would tell all my friends and family to get their sympathy and support. I would then empower myself by leaving the relationship and lick my wounds while searching for a better relationship. Eventually, I would get into another relationship with a different person in different circumstances, but inevitably, it would end with the same destructive results.

I absolutely had to find a way to empower myself without inviting my issues of abandonment, rejection, and betrayal into my relationships. The problem with the scenario of choosing to leave the relationship to empower myself meant that to continue to feel empowered, I would have to repeat the same game repeatedly.

I wanted to liberate myself from this unending cycle and find a healthier way of empowerment. I needed to heal the core issue from my past from which my beliefs of inadequacy had begun. I had to regress to the point where it had originated and heal it from there.

The process was not easy. What would have been easy was to listen to my family and friends and leave the relationship while pointing the finger at my partner and coming out of the situation smelling like a rose, rather than taking responsibility for my part in the circumstances, which was that I attracted the situation out of my unhealed wounds and would continue to attract similar situations until I changed my core beliefs about myself and heal.

I had to get to the point at which the pain of staying stuck and repeating my patterns was greater than my fear of feeling my emotions and healing. Gratefully, I had enough self-love guiding me through this process, and I reached out for help.

I found my core betrayal, the incident where it all had begun. From my experience and through working with others, I've found it is usually somewhere in the first seven years of our lives. I also had a past-life regression and found the lifetime where I'd died unhealed, with betrayal in my heart. This is a procedure that takes assistance from someone who knows how to heal. I found the core beliefs that handicapped my emotional field, and I changed them. The beliefs I held on to and finally healed were the feelings that I am not good enough, it is not safe to speak my truth, and I am not important.

After I changed my past debilitating core beliefs into "I am good enough," "it is safe to speak my truth," and "I am important," all my relationships changed. Now I am no longer afraid of abandonment, rejection, and betrayal, and because I stopped attracting these situations to me, the spell was finally broken, and I learned to liberate and empower myself through self-love.

I am not holding on to the anger. I am allowing the anger to open and flow in a way that brings me closer to my truth. I am allowing it to show me where I have betrayed myself, and I am building a bridge to understand unconditional love for myself. I am accepting the way my partner betrayed me and accepting his human fallibility while also holding him accountable to his own journey of growth.

I do not want to be just empowered; I want to go beyond it. Liberation and empowerment are the gift of loving despite all the drama and difficulties. It is having control over not what other people do but rather what I do. It is not about anger, wrath, or discouragement but about breaking the mold and going beyond. It is about believing that self-love conquers more than I can ever conceive possible and knowing that love exists in all people, even when they make bad choices. I know that Source has a plan for me in the grand scheme of things even when I cannot see beyond the clouds.

It is not about deciding which relationship stays or goes; it is about how I conduct my love in the relationship. Can I respect and love myself despite what other people choose to do? Can I be filled with empowerment knowing that love is the greatest power life has given to me? Can I love in this struggle by knowing who I am and what I came here to do and continue learning to love deeper as part of my journey?

"I love because my love is not dependent on the object of my love. My love is dependent on my state of being. So, whether the other person changes or becomes different, friend turns into foe, it does not matter, because my love was never dependent on the other person. My love is my state of being. I simply love." Osho

Being a wounded healer means understanding the value of one's pain, having the courage to investigate its purpose, and choosing liberation over victimization. Taking responsibility (ability-to-respond) means learning the lesson and changing the behavior. If I am still behaving the same, then it is not old behavior.

Liberation becomes the process of breaking free from a cycle, mold, and chain that binds us. All we have to do is ask for liberation, and in the process of choosing something different, we become free.

PART II

CHAPTER 8

Forgiving the Unforgivable

Sometimes it takes an overwhelming breakdown to have an
undeniable breakthrough.
—author unknown

Be the person who breaks the cycle. If you were judged, choose
understanding. If you were rejected, choose acceptance. If you were
shamed, choose compassion. Be the person you needed when you were
hurting, not the person who hurt you. Vow to be better than what
broke you—to heal instead of becoming biter so you can act from your
heart, not your pain.
—Lori Deschene

Our misuse of personal power comes from not understanding its purpose, value, and strength. Many of us were victims of circumstances for so long that during our recovery process, we never imagined what our lives could look like healed, whole, and perfect. Some of us choose to stay in the limbo stage of victimhood because it is what we were taught, and we continue to recite learned behavior. Besides, as described in the previous chapter, victimhood can offer safety and familiarity that is nurturing, socially acceptable, and even educational if we choose to go to therapy.

Some of us are ready to take risks and jump over the abyss of dark repression in which victim consciousness holds us hostage and begin to live creative lives because the ties of captivity are only an illusion, a held perception, and a borrowed belief system that can be changed. Life defines us by the choices we make and not by our intentions.

Wounded healers and warriors of the dark night of the soul are people who contracted with the board of karma before birth to undergo specific trauma, challenges, and even abuse in this incarnation. Some do this to correct past karma; nevertheless, the path of the healer and warrior is not to become or stay a victim but to overcome these adversities in order to heal oneself and others. Healers are spiritual warriors who have found the courage to defeat the shadow side of their souls, awakening and rising from the depths of their deepest fears, like a phoenix rising from the ashes. These individuals are reborn with wisdom, vitality, and strength, creating a light shining bright enough to help, encourage, and inspire others out of their own darkness.

From my experience and observations, I know this process is profound. Past-life healing and soul awareness let us evolve faster. When we heal the wounds that are constantly repeating through this life, we gain more guidance and awareness. In one lifetime, we have the ability to heal hundreds of versions of ourselves, past and future. Healing ourselves and breaking old patterns allows us to release and free the family legacy. This includes our ancestors, past and future generations, and children from suffering these patterns. This is one of the most powerful healing transformations going on with our planet right now. We are here to awaken to this potentiometer, clear these lives, and birth a new earth—a place where people thrive in love, awareness, and soul healing. The salvation of humanity starts with self.

In Egyptian numerology, the last name is called the hereditary name. It is the numerology passed down through generations. It shows us what our family histories have carried energetically for hundreds of years. This will be discussed in part 4 of this book under chapter 19, "Sacred Oracle Word."

Besides faith and confidence, one of the elements we lose when we are hurting is the ability to trust. We can close ourselves off from every lifeline of help available to us, doubt our intuition, lose faith in the world around us, and at times even doubt our own self-worth, but without trust, we separate and isolate ourselves by becoming an island without a harbor. This may be necessary for a while in the healing process, but it absolutely cannot stay as a permanent place of residence. At some point in time, we need to learn to trust again. For me, I allowed my relationship with nature to open my heart again.

One of the toughest hurdles I have had to climb is the rebuilding of trust. I thought it would be easier and safer to become a recluse than to trust again. I spent a lot of my younger years in nature rather than in social groups because I found I could always trust nature. Natural disasters may not be easy to predict, but I can accept them; nature never lied to me and is always what it appears to be. As I grew older, it was necessary for me to seek outside help for many of life's problems, and so my journey to allow people to help me began once again. But I needed to be in a lot of pain before I would soften, surrender, and be vulnerable enough to ask for help.

Trust is a bridge from one person to another person, place, or thing. I used to think it was built mutually between two people, but I no longer hold that belief. My trust in someone can be established, strengthened, and destroyed entirely by my own will. Its existence depends on my expectations, needs, or an established agreement that serves me. When there is an outside person, place, or thing involved, there are no longer guarantees, and all rules are subject to change. There is always a risk.

I can even trust myself at 110 percent, but I am wise enough now to allow the freedom to change my mind, opinion, beliefs, and perception from time to time as necessary for internal growth. How many times have you watched a movie where one of the main characters says to his or her lover, "I will never leave you!" and then gets hit by a car? So, for better or for worse, there are no guarantees in life except the love, guidance, and support from Higher Source. This is the only sure thing that I know of today that is not subject to change. My experience is that when you love and trust someone, make sure you are leaving enough room for life's little surprises because life happens when you're not looking. Do not get blindsided by adopting rigid rules, and be sure to install windows that allow you a view with a great sense of humor.

Gaining back the trust of my intuition was something worth fighting for and one of the greatest rewards in the healing process because I passionately believe that great power comes to those who listen to the whispers of their spirits instead of the noise of the world. Those who follow the guidance provided by their intuition walk through doorways of peace, positivity, prosperity, and compassion. Learn to listen, and most importantly, learn to trust your intuition.

When You Change the Way You Look at Things, the Things You Look at Change

"There are no guarantees," "life's not fair," and "things are not always going to be easy breezy" are phrases I did not identify with growing up. *Surely, they jest. Those rules apply to everyone but me,* I thought. After all, isn't life what you make it? I suffered from an entitlement complex, which is a grand state of mind when staying focused on a goal but does nothing for the acceptance of reality in general. When growing up, we all get sold on the fantasy that life is going to be easy, and it hurts like hell to learn the truth.

I remember being in a pit of despair when my therapist asked me the fatal life-turning question, "Where did you learn that life was fair?" OMG, I had a field day with that question. He basically left me speechless as I glazed over, in my mind searching for the answer to his question. I thought hard about it for the following two weeks. I had such a strong sense of internal justice sitting on a throne somewhere within me. I just knew that there was something that told me what was right and wrong, but I could not remember *where* it came from.

That was the beginning of my self-examination of belief systems that I myself had not installed. I had to examine the difference between what I knew was right and wrong and what I had been taught. Was what I knew and what I was taught in alignment with my truth? All this self-examination was stirring up the dust covering my peace of mind. I started to question many things that I believed to be true, had even defended, only to find out that the more I learned, the less I knew.

I finally admitted complete defeat that he—my therapist—was right; there are no guarantees, life is not fair, and it is not always easy. *So now what? Where do I go from here?* The answer is exactly where the path took me—to humility, surrender, and acceptance: "Get off the cross; we need the wood."

The biggest truth that I questioned was my ability to control life and how the outside world controlled me. I know I do not have control over people, places, things, and circumstances outside myself. If life is not fair, easy, or guaranteed, then I am 100 percent sure that I have absolutely no control over outside influences. I do, however, have control over my body, heart, mind, and spirit and how I react to circumstances. The divine paradox is that the outside world is always a reflection of what is going on inside of me. Now, these are the things they did not teach me in school—that everything going on outside my life is but a mere reflection of my inner self.

> Remember that your perception of the world is a reflection of your state of consciousness. (Eckhart Tolle)

The law of attraction comes into play because we attract what is on our radar from an energetic point of view, and our fears qualify under this umbrella. Abandonment, rejection, and betrayal are the most popular victim portals that we all carry with us at one point of time or another, and they can be handed down to us through past-life events or our parents' belief systems, or we can acquire these as new behaviors. How many times have you said, "Well, this is just who I am," and then tried to find people to work around your deficiencies? No more, nope, not going to work. It is time for us to clean up and take responsibility for our energy, serenity, and well-being.

If everything reflects our own energy, then true forgiveness must come from having compassion toward ourselves, and if we take full responsibility for our energy and what we attract, we are the ones who must learn self-love before we change any outside circumstances. Unless we learn to face our own shadows and demons, we will continue to see them in others, because the world outside us is always a reflection of the world inside us. We are affecting the world every moment, whether we realize it or not. Our feelings, actions, and state of mind matter because we are so deeply interconnected with one another, working on our own consciousness is the most important thing that we are doing at any given moment, and being love is the supreme creative act. If we keep avoiding self-love, the universe will keep sending us people who also avoid loving us, hoping we get the message.

Nothing ever truly leaves until it has taught us what we need to learn. The universe does not give us what we want because it is too busy giving us what we need. It will use various means necessary to get our attention, including loss, grief, death, illness, and even the people we love. It finds ways to surface what we have hidden in the depths of our souls that needs to be remembered, discovered, and acted on. It continually emerges into our consciousness all the things we need to address, learn, and heal so that we ultimately can reach our ordained destinies.

Forgiving the unforgivable means that, in life, there really is nothing outside myself to forgive. If everything happens for a reason and the outside world is a reflection of what is going within me, then it is my responsibility to love and forgive myself, find the lesson, allow acceptance, and let go of the drama. In fact, I often replace the word *forgiveness* with the phrase *acceptance with a touch of grace* and then recite the serenity prayer.

God, grant me the serenity to accept the things I cannot change (you)

The courage to change the things I can (me)
And the wisdom to know the difference
(Reinhold Hiebuhr)

By following this prayer, I have learned to live a peaceful and balanced way of life. Whenever there is something I cannot accept in my life, I pray for the wisdom to know the difference and the correct action to take.

<u>CHAPTER 9</u>

Nobody Deserves Forgiveness—That is Why God Gave Us Grace

When you find no solution to a problem, it is not a problem to be solved but a truth to be accepted.

One thing we learn while staying in alignment with our soul-life agreements is that time is not our friend and does not heal all wounds. This is a twisted myth, and whenever I hear this statement, I want to scream.

Time is not a healer, and some realists may argue that time is an illusion. The implication that time heals wounds can be a dangerous trap because it suggests that we avoid our feelings and move on while this magical force called *time* will eventually take our troubles away.

In numerology, time is a measuring tool. It measures maturation, cycles, and transformation and can be split open to uncover portals. It does not heal. We become the healers because we are the key components to the healing process.

To my knowledge and experience, it is the acts of self-love, compassion, and acceptance that heal all wounds. To stay and be in alignment with our journeys, we understand that all healing stems from our ability to love ourselves deeply and to surround ourselves with people who support us.

I have had to heal some incredible pain in my life, and when I allowed time to heal, it basically diverted my issues into addiction. This is where I learned that time does not have a medical license or PhD in psychology. The value of being a wounded healer always points to self-love and our willingness to venture through the unknown to learn valuable lessons about who we are and why we came here. Time is irrelevant.

The only way out of the darkness is by allowing ourselves to travel within. Exploring every crevice of our existence and acquainting ourselves with our inner demons allows us to understand why they have taken residency within our minds and feast on our spirits. We must train them to stop filling our thoughts with toxic habitual ways and force them to recognize that they have been suffocating our true identities, poisoning us with hate, and blinding us from seeing our truth. It takes us hard work and patience before they surrender to our demands, but we must keep persisting and never let hope slip from our grasp, even when they try to convince us that darkness is where we reside.

Eventually, they will have no choice but to step aside so we can once again discover the radiance of our own beings, feel the elation as they swirl around our bodies, and embrace the surge of passion as our hearts begins to pump love throughout our veins. This is when we know we have successfully defeated the demons of darkness, unearthed our inner warriors, and discovered the radiating light of our own existence. We can now confidently go through life knowing we have the wisdom of light to guide us as we walk down our destined paths.

This process often takes us through the darkness and leads us on a journey into the light—a journey from darkness into the strength and hidden resources of our souls. Navigating the dark requires interior dialogue, contemplation, prayer, quiet time, and sharing with those who understand and value the profound nature of inner transformation.

When we are in this interior place, we stand at the crossroads of our power, between our ego and our soul, between time and timelessness. Like butterflies rising out of their cocoons, we become the miraculous healers.

Before we can gain true power and wisdom from our experiences, we must enter the chambers of forgiveness. How do we begin to forgive the unforgivable? Forgiveness has nothing to do with the other person, place, thing, or circumstance. It has everything to do with ourselves and the damage that has occurred on all levels of our existence because of harm done from another source. Something happened that hurt us terribly, and in honor of our sacred beings, it must be acknowledged. No matter what it was, it feels terrible, and it is a deep wound. Forgiveness offers the wounded eternal peace.

The wound must be identified, and the feelings that haunt us must be felt. Nobody deserves to experience a violation, and this is part of the imbalance occurring in our energy fields. It takes an enormous amount of self-love and compassion to overcome these dark entities, and people are not meant to defeat their demons alone. If I had not experienced victory over mine, I would not think or know it to be possible.

Forgiveness is a process that starts with asking for help because liberation is for the asking. We must be ready and at the point of being sick and tired of holding on to anger and resentment from lack of justice. To be honest, I enjoy holding on to anger sometimes because I thrive on the adrenaline. I always get my chores done in half the time, it pumps me up, and it makes me feel powerful. This is dangerous behavior, for self-righteous indignation is a double-edged sword.

Self-love and self-respect lead us in the right direction if action is needed to bring justice to our circumstances. If there is nothing that can be done and the feeling of being uncomfortable persists, forgiveness is the right action. The dark qualities that hold a victim captive will eventually take its toll. Experiencing disease or illness and becoming the abuser are highly likely in the long run because it is a known fact that hurt people will hurt people. We may eventually become the very thing that we despise.

Many of us feel a quality of shame after we have been abused. We feel that somehow it was our fault and that maybe we could have prevented it, stopped it, fought back, and changed the circumstances in one way or another. I personally felt unworthy, lower than the earth, and unlovable. Even though this does not make rational sense, it is still how many of us feel after being victims of abuse. I know I felt this way for many years.

I was only twelve years old, but I thought that somehow it was my fault for being abducted by racial gang members and sexually, emotionally, mentally, and physically tortured. These people threatened my life and the lives of my family members if I went to the police. They promised to burn our house down; stalked me day and night, putting dead animals in my mailbox; and even went to my school, threatening me at knifepoint.

A few months after the incident, my girlfriend and I were walking the schoolyard after class, and I saw the group of the boys who'd violated me playing basketball. They were going on with life as though nothing had happened to me. Their lives continued while mine was ruined.

I felt an overwhelming sadness that these people lived such shallow lives. Their goals in life consisted of belonging to a rowdy, senseless gang who drank away promising dreams and overpowering women to feel a sense of accomplishment. Their souls were lifeless and lost. Their futures drowned in repeating cultural patterns. What a tremendous loss of gifts they had been given to succeed in life, and they had no idea how rich their potential could be.

Something beyond my control took over my mind and body. I left my friend standing at edge of the building shadows, as I was being magnetically pulled to walk right in the middle of their game.

Maybe a part of me felt that the worst they could do was kill me, and after all I had been through, I often welcomed physical death. I really had nothing left to lose, and I had something I needed to share with them.

The basketball dropped and rolled off to the side of the court as they circled around me. I intuitively started backing off, but the words came spilling out. "I feel sorry for all you. Your minds and hearts are closed to your full potential. There is so much more to life than drinking and raping women, and if you continue down this path, it will lead you nowhere. You think that this little town is all there is, but there are beautiful places in this world. You don't have to stay here, and what you think is normal for your age would be considered barbaric and just sad in other parts of our country."

I could feel their anger swell around me. And the circle grew tighter. I thought they were going to beat me. Just as the tension peaked, I heard a car horn. I turned around and saw my father's old Ford pickup truck parked along the road. He called my name, and I escaped without harm.

That summer, our family moved back to our hometown. Two years later, when I was fifteen years old, I received a letter from two of my perpetrators. In this letter, they apologized for how they'd treated me and thanked me for my words of encouragement. They wanted me to know that they had taken my advice and they both joined the navy in San Diego, far away from their little hometown of despair and destruction. They abandoned their lives as gang members and were now living lives of service for their country and had dreams for their futures.

I thanked the universe for notifying me that maybe something good had come out of my suffering. Maybe I'd helped to save a few lives that might have been demolished had these men continued down their dark paths. How many women will never have to be victimized—and maybe, just maybe, these men developed their potential gifts and are contributing to the world instead of destroying the light.

I held on to this secret for fifteen years, and in the meantime, I hid my fear, anxiety, and pain beneath alcohol and drug use. I started acting out in unhealthy ways, and it affected my relationships with other people and eventually my occupation. I was twenty-eight (my Saturn return) before I finally sought help for all the anguish that had led to my addictions. I asked for help, allowed the healing process to begin, cleaned up, and found a set of spiritual principles to live by. The one thing I had to learn was to *forgive myself.* It sounds ridiculous because I did nothing wrong, but I forgave myself anyways.

Empower yourself through self-forgiveness.

<u>CHAPTER 10</u>

Forgive Yourself

Don't run from your Demons; learn their Names
—Charles Bukowski

Self-love cannot be sustained without forgiveness, acceptance, and a touch of grace. We must forgive ourselves and those who have hurt us, as when we choose to forgive those who hurt us, we take away their power. This does not mean we forget the pain; we just find a way to use it to fuel our purpose. Letting go of the hurt will allow us to focus on being whole, authentic, and present. Using our challenges as lessons allows us to write new chapters to our stories that inspire, so we can emerge better, not bitter. When we forgive ourselves, we no longer hold ourselves hostage to versions of our past shadows that no longer exist.

Forgive yourself for allowing bad things to happen to you. Many of us were children. Forgive yourself for being vulnerable, open, and innocent. There is nothing wrong with being innocent. Forgive yourself.

Many of us were overpowered physically, emotionally, and mentally. Forgive yourself for being at the wrong place at the wrong time. You were only practicing your right of personal freedom. Forgive yourself.

Some of us were held against our will while we were practicing our right to be safe. You have a right to be safe. Forgive yourself.

Many of us have been lied to and had promises broken while we were practicing trust and faithfulness. You deserve honesty and an open heart. Forgive yourself.

Some of us have been deceived and manipulated while we were practicing friendship. You are worthy of true partnership. Forgive yourself.

Forgive yourself for the time you could not release something because you needed it to survive.

Forgive yourself for whatever happened, even for the mistakes and poor choices you have made, for not showing up the way you needed to, and for not being the person you wanted to be. You are human.

You did the best you could in the moment given with what you knew and what you had to work with at that time; that is all you can ask of yourself. You are still learning, still growing, and still finding your way. All this takes time, and you can give yourself that time. You are allowed to show up in the world imperfectly. You can fail at things that you tried so hard to achieve. You are allowed to realize that you made wrong decisions and become someone who is still figuring out their path and purpose.

Most of all, you are allowed to forgive yourself.

You cannot go back and change the decisions you once made, but you can choose what you do today, and you can keep choosing again and again. You can always start over, and this is where your power is—in today.

No more beating yourself up and going over and over it again in your head, torturing yourself with the past. What happened, happened, and all the shame, regret, and self-hatred in the world will not undo that.

Today, you are beginning new.

Today, you are moving forward in life with new knowledge and experiences you have gathered. You can be the person you want to be and live the life you want to live. You are not a bad person, a disappointment, or a failure. You are human. You are still learning, growing, and finding your way ... and it is all OK.

Eventually, we will look back on our previous lives of indulgence as adults looking back on the ignorance of their youth, without judgment or condemnation but with a healthy sense of regret and compassion for the previous delusions.

Perpetrators, victims, or victors, we all have a part in our traumas. Forgiveness is the vehicle to true power, as it opens our hearts, minds, and energy fields and warrants against disease. If we continue to hold on to our anger, fear, and negativity, we continue to attract those events and circumstances that keep us captive and hostage until we finally dissolve them once and for all. This is a universal law, and there are no exceptions. We are meant to overcome them, and forgiveness is our parachute.

When I swam in the tar pit from the dark-night-of-the-soul circumstances, I was angry with Source. "How could a loving, kind, and compassionate God allow a human being to feel so bad and still be alive?" What I did not realize for a long time is that Source gave me enough power, light, and wisdom to heal myself and the world. I found that this Source is not in the darkness business but in the light-and-love business, and when I asked for help, it arrived.

I had to stop asking, "Why did this happen to me?" and start asking, "How can I live in the solution?"

I felt compelled to have to understand why bad things were happening to me until one day a friend told me to ask Source for help. She told me that I may never understand why bad things happen the way they do but that I can ask for help and live in the solution rather than dwell in the problem.

It is not my job to understand everything anymore. I used to have a strong desire to understand everything until I realized that my need to understand was fear based. If I could understand a situation, then I could manipulate it, and if I could manipulate it, then I could control it. If I could control all the situations happening in my life, then maybe I would never get hurt again. It was not until I admitted that I am completely powerless over people, places, and circumstances before I was willing to let go of trying to control the events in my life and begin to trust in a power greater than myself.

What I learned is to not try to understand everything, because sometimes it is meant not to be understood but to be accepted.

Now I am satisfied to learn about synchronicities, symmetry, symbols, and signs. This is the way Source communicates with me today. I resonate with the harmonies of the universe, including the elementals, animals, nature, and our environment. I am not obsessed with having to understand everything, because I desire to resonate. I do not dominate; I blend. I rise above duality, and I disappear with acceptance and allowance. All this is accomplished with love, appreciation, respect, and honor because creating is the universe's business today, and I trust the world in its hands. I trust in grace and forgive the illusion of separation so I may awaken to the truth of Oneness.

Buddhist Prayer of Forgiveness

If I have harmed anyone in any way either knowingly
or unknowingly through my own confusions, I ask
their forgiveness. If anyone has harmed me in any
way either knowingly or unknowingly through their
own confusions, I forgive them. And if there is a
situation, I am not yet ready to forgive, I forgive
myself for that. For all the ways that I harm, negate,
doubt, belittle, judge, or be unkind to myself through
my own confusions, I forgive myself.

<u>CHAPTER 11</u>

The Brighter the Light, the Darker the Shadow

Forgive others, not because they deserve forgiveness,
but because you deserve peace.
—Jonathan Lockwood Huie

Every time we embody more light, it brings up unprocessed emotions and situations still needing to be shifted from our pasts. We take a breath and then take a few steps back to transcend the stuck energy. We are not regressing, because this is part of our personal-growth process.

It is a known theory that whenever we are dawning closer to the light of higher wisdom and our life purposes, the darkness cowers around us, using this opportunity to vacuum the light back into the shadows of the abyss and the unknown. The darkness never fails a chance to discourage the enlightened. It makes us doubt ourselves around every corner, creates havoc, and uproots our emotional balance until we hardly recognize ourselves. When this begins to happen, we intuitively know we are on the right path. One of the strongest pitfalls to resist is resentment.

The Buddha referred to holding on to resentment and anger as grasping a hot coal with the intent of throwing it at someone else. The one who holds the resentment gets burned in the process. Unresolved anger and hurt feelings are not only the cause of disease but a self-made prison, holding captive the demons of destruction and allowing them to wreak havoc on our personal souls. If we are the victims of others' ill behavior, decisions, and actions, the last thing we need to do is punish ourselves for their sins. In the karmic realm of cause and effect, nothing goes unnoticed. Holding on to resentment, not clearing it, only guarantees a situational return until we get it right. These are universal laws. Retaliation, revenge, and punishment are just methods we use to play God, but they have undesirable consequences, and if we do not respond to healing our wounds, this too has undesirable consequences. People do not want to hear the truth, because they do not want their illusions shattered, and the greatest illusion is that humankind has limitations.

Taking the high ground is the safest way to keep out of the emotional floods of depression, but it brings us back to the question of, how do we forgive the unforgivable? My father cheated on my mother, and I watched her live a lonely unresolved life. Because she did not overcome her loss and heal her wounds, she passed this legacy on by teaching me her behaviors. Do I close myself off, stop trusting, and keep this havoc unresolved only to pass the same fate on to my daughter? This is my motivation for healing my wounds besides healing myself. I do not want my daughter to have to suffer my unresolved consequences. So, I am willing to take the bull by the horns and dissolve this ongoing momentum of family repression and ancestral prognosis. It is time to ask myself, "Where did these beliefs about who I am come from, and how old are they?" Updating my identity became crucial to my evolution and life purpose.

Disappointment is just an un-birthed resentment. I used to say I did not have any resentments, but I was sure disappointed about a lot of things! I was so unhappy because I carried my list of disappointments in a backpack with me wherever I went. When my therapist asked me to list all my disappointments, they came out smelling like resentments. He asked me how much control I thought I had over other people, places, and things. My new assignment was to go thirty days without saying "I am sorry," judging myself or others, and saying the words *could* or *should* in a sentence. When I reported back to him in the following two weeks, I told him that if I was not doing at least one of these things, there was nothing left for me to do. I became bored very quickly.

He was trying to show me how much spare time I would have if I did not waste all my time on disappointments and resentments. I took the long way around that lesson, but I finally learned.

> Waking up to who we are requires letting go of who
> we imagine ourselves to be (Alan Watts)

When I work with people, we spend time clearing energy leaks and disappointments. This frees up our energy so we can focus on what we came here to do, because our lives have purpose, our stories are important, our dreams count, and we were born to make an impact. We were made to explore, experience, and expand ... again and again! The universe displays itself as fractal, meaning that whatever energy resonance we carry will be repeated infinitely until we change the vibration.

<u>CHAPTER 12</u>

Reflections

Change is Inevitable, but Transformation is by Conscious Choice
—HeatherAsh Amara

We use affirmations to develop certain key attitudes pertaining to self-concept and self-image. Every thought and feeling we allow into our minds is an affirmation and visualization, and once accepted into the conscious mind, it imprints itself on the subconscious mind like a tape recorder or computer and then attracts and magnetizes it! The subconscious mind is always attracting and magnetizing, so we need to choose what we allow it to magnetize and attract.

Now the question is, why do affirmations and visualizations not always get the results people want? First, we realize that every thought we think, feeling we feel, word we speak, and action we take is an affirmation and that people are doing affirmations and visualizations every moment of their lives. Second, people need to be aware of all the programming that currently exists in their subconscious minds from this lifetime and all other past lives. Third, most people do not have 100 percent mastery of their thoughts, emotions, negative ego minds, lower-self desires, and inner child and are not always thinking and feeling with their divine minds.

When light workers use positive affirmations and visualizations, however, they are having to counteract an enormous amount of programming that is already functioning as an affirmation and visualization and all the positive or negative daily self-talk that is the inner dialogue that goes on all day in everyone's consciousness. The positive affirmations and visualizations definitely help, but we need to clean out our subconscious minds; work on gaining full mastery of daily thinking, feeling, speaking, negative egos, the inner child, lower-self desires, and so on.

Above all else, we must keep any thought not of Source from entering our minds!

This is the golden key to life and manifestation.

Reflections are direct intentions we learn to embody. When the universe receives this energy, we attract the same energy we are transmitting.

We use our intention to take back our light, and once we understand how the universe works, we have the power to get the universe to work for us.

Everything in the universe is vibrating at a particular frequency and every individual has a unique resonance vibration. Our thoughts and feelings, including everything in our subconscious, are transmitting this vibration out into the universe, and those vibrations shape the lives we are living.

This is how the universe works.

When our energy vibrates at a frequency that is in direct alignment with what the universe has been attempting to deliver to us our entire lives, we begin to live in the flow where true miracles begin to appear.

When we heal trauma, we heal the nervous system. When we heal the nervous system, we heal the emotional body. When the emotional body is healed, then the psychic, or empathic, body heals, and when we heal our psychic bodies, we heal our vibrations. Once the vibration is healed, realities shift and change.

If we are feeling stuck, unfulfilled, or dissatisfied with life, the answer lies in raising our personal vibrations to a higher pitch, where our intentions and desires resonate with the positive energy that the universe recognizes and delivers back to us.

The creation frequency is that sweet spot when we are in tune with the flow in life. When we tap into this frequency, we reclaim the creative power that is waiting for us to receive, and we find ourselves working in partnership with the universe to work toward our intended outcomes rather than incidental ones.

If everything in the universe is energy, then the things we want are less like solid objects and more like currents of frequency that we can redirect toward ourselves. We direct energy to create intentions through the vibrations of our desires and our thoughts. What we focus on becomes our realities, and where attention goes, energy flows.

Consider all possible outcomes as flowing radio frequencies, where each one has its own personal vibration and outcome, and we are the antennas sending and receiving these signals all the time. We use our intentions to focus on the reflection frequencies that we desire and then tune in.

The outer world is a direct reflection of our inner worlds, and now is the time to be acutely aware of our thought patterns and let go of those that no longer serve us. No need to let old ways of thinking and operating weigh us down anymore. The fears we do not walk through become walls that keep us from moving forward, and there has never been a better time to clean up our energy and choose positivity. When we are kind, happy, and at peace within, we start to see more of those things reflected to us through our relationships and experiences. We may run into challenges, but it is how we choose to react to them that makes the difference.

The universe does not give us the people we want; it gives us the people we need—the ones who will help, hurt, leave, and love us to make us the individuals we were designed to be. And when we replace "Why is this happening to me?" with "What is this trying to teach me?" everything shifts.

This is our world to create, so let us make it a miraculous one.

The Twelve Reflections

Silence Is Golden / Words Are Vibrations / Thoughts Are Creation

We are Spirit, primordial, self-propelling, self-sustaining, intelligent eternal energy. Everything is a matter of energy, from raising in frequency, higher awareness, manifestations, and life changes to comprehension of truth. So the crux is to understand how to work with our energy and not waste it. Energy is talked about much, but seemingly few understand it and know how to work with it.

The twelve reflections are affirmation statements used to enhance our energy centers. When we align our chakras, we raise our energy fields, and our inner reflections attract the outer manifestations of greatness.

Law of attraction, universal truths, and karmic lessons can all be understood through the looking glass of these twelve reflections.

We become what we believe. Here are some reflections and affirmations to replace those beliefs that no longer serve us:

1. **We are all one (root chakra):** We are unlimited love, light, and consciousness with free will, and we are created equal. "I breathe into the base of my spine, creating an opening for strength, stability, courage, and secure solid foundation in every area of my life."

2. **Honor one another (sacral chakra):** We are all reflections of one another and honor ourselves and others with love, compassion, and understanding. Treat everyone the way you want to be treated, and take responsibility for everything in your life, because it all belongs to you. "I breathe into this space to create an opening for the energy of sacred relationships, flow of emotions without guilt and shame, freedom to be myself, and the enjoyment of sacred pleasure."

3. **I am a divine creator (solar plexus chakra):** We are powerful and passionate and obtain the ability to create beauty within and without. "I breathe into this space to create an opening for the energy of expansion for my personal power, spiritual growth, and strong sense of self-worth, knowing that I am a powerful creator."

4. **I am the power of acceptance and grace (lower heart chakra):** Good judgment comes from experience, and experience comes from bad judgment. Our feelings are like visitors; they were never meant to stay and camp out. Our thoughts are like clouds, which are meant to drift in and then out of our minds. "I breathe into this

space to create an opening for the fires of transformation to burn through everything unsettled and transmute into acceptance and grace."

5. **Love is divine power (heart center chakra):** I love unconditionally because I choose to be without expectations. Expectations are only premeditated resentments. If we refuse to repeat an experience, then we learn to face our fears, invite them to the table, and make peace with them. "I breathe into this space to create an opening for energy to clear so that I can live with passion, accept emotions, give and receive unconditionally, and feel deeply connected to all that is."

6. **I am grateful (higher heart chakra):** Be grateful for everything good, bad, and indifferent. Everything is here as a lesson to teach, test, and motivate us. Accept the lessons and the blessings. "I breathe into this space to create an opening of higher love to activate my deep gratitude for spiritual freedom, love, peace, serenity, tranquility, and joy that is abundant and always flowing through me."

7. **I speak my highest truth (throat chakra):** Love yourself enough to always speak your truth. Be in integrity by walking your talk, and treasure the spoken word. "I breathe into the space that lets me create an opening to the energy of truth. I express myself without fear, and I speak words that uplift, inspire, and are aligned with the vibration of the highest spiritual good for all."

8. **I seek my highest truth (third eye):** Be a seeker of divine knowledge. Do not settle for anything but the truth in every situation. "I breathe into the space that creates an opening so that I may accept my own clairvoyance to clearly see my soul path—to trust my inner knowing completely, without reservation, surrendering to that voice, the voice that is guiding me to my greatest good."

9. **I open my portal of dreams (zeal point):** Use your imagination daily, daydream, night dream, record, and follow these insights wherever they take you. "I breathe into this space that creates an opening to the higher realms revealing their secrets through my dreams and imagination. I ask this portal to always be open, available, and protected as I journey to the outer realms."

10. **I am a community healer/leader (tripod point):** Become a light worker/warrior. "I breathe through this space that creates an opening for me to greet my higher self and activate my gifts of healing, uniting my path, purpose, and destiny while manifesting wisdom through higher truths."

11. **I am open to the divine (crown chakra):** Keep open only to the Divine, and ask the angels for protection. "I breathe into the space that creates an opening to Universal Life Force, allowing it to pour into me; ignite my highest spiritual understanding and knowledge of self; and flow unobstructed throughout all the chakras,

illuminating perfect health, purity, peace, love, and joy that I am."

12. **I am supported, guided, and loved:** "I Invite the ascended masters, animals spirits, and all beings, souls and spirits seen and unseen, serving the love, light, beauty, power, grace, and truth of Source to guide, guard, and protect me at all times."

Lakota Prayer

Great Mystery,
teach me how to trust
my heart, my mind, my intuition,
my inner knowing,
the senses of my body,
the blessings of my spirit.
Teach me to trust these things
so that I may enter my sacred space
and love beyond my fear
and walk in balance
with the passing of each glorious sun.

<u>CHAPTER 13</u>

Energy Codes of Honor and Fake Healers

Nothing I've been taught is unadjustable to the truth.

We are all healers, but most of us never tap into and acknowledge our power. When we connect to our souls, we connect to collective consciousness, and when we are connected to the collective, we are connected to everything. That is how we know, feel, see, hear, touch, and taste beyond our five physical senses—because we are able to perceive the oneness. We are not limited to one body, person, thought, place, or time. This is powerful beyond measure; it is the omnipotence of the soul.

I live in Sedona, Arizona, where healers, psychics, and artists are a dime a dozen. From my experience, I can count on one hand how many true authentic healers and psychics practice here. In reality, we are all healers and psychics, and anyone who claims to be more special than the rest of us is basically on an ego trip. We do not become psychics, healers, and channels simply because we already are from the day we are born. As we learn to uncover our innate abilities, we practice principles and develop our gifts.

You can identify fake healers by many characteristics, but the most common fake healers are the ones who separate themselves from the community, proclaiming that they are conduits to Spirit and need to keep their psyches pure. This will imply that the rest of us are impure and will contaminate these gifted souls simply by being in their presence. The frustration with this behavior is the act of separation and the implication that the rest of us belong to an impure population. In this manner, they become the healers, and we are the sick ones.

For some reason, this action is rationalized and accepted in their occupational circumstances. I have to ask, "What would have happened if Jesus healed in this manner?"

How authentic can healers and psychics be if they are afraid to see their own reflections in other people? Are they too sensitive to heal their own shadows or afraid to uncover what the rest of us are seeking, which is the truth? Too many healers and psychics keep people in the problem so they will become dependent on them, and this condition is fear and ego based, which can be dangerous. So please be aware of any healers and psychics who separate themselves and consider themselves specially assigned from Higher Source to your bidding.

What follows is a list that I call *the energy code of honor*. I am sharing with you some of the most important aspects of raising our energy levels. It has to do with the universal laws of energy. It is vital to know that there is a responsibility that comes with being a keeper of the light. Some people tend to consider themselves special, above the normal, and different once their frequencies shift. We begin to notice that we attract people, places, and things faster by merely focusing our attention on our desires. It is therefore critical to direct our thoughts with consideration not only for ourselves but for others, and before we heal others, it is important to ask if they are willing to give up the things that made them sick.

> Compassion is not a relationship between the healer and the wounded, it is a relationship between equals. Only when we know our own darkness well, can we be present with the darkness of others. Compassion becomes real when we recognize our shared humanity. (Pema Chodron)

1. **Law of attraction:** As light workers, we direct immense healing powers. We will be attracted to situations that require our support. We must decide with our inner guidance and intuition whether we are qualified to get involved in specific situations. We may be asked to walk people and animals through painful situations, and sometimes we may need the assistance of others. We must take caution not to overextend our qualifications and always ask for assistance if we are not sure.

2. **Law of discernment:** Do no harm. We are not entitled to use our powers for selfish gain at the expense of others. If we use our energy to feed our egos, we will lose our power until it is corrected. Some people see themselves beyond this law, but once we lower our standards, our light and energy also withdraw. If we continue without correction or pardon, our future powers will diminish and possibly become a delusion.

3. **Law of reflection:** Avoid judgment and turning anyone away who needs healing. We are all reflections for one another. I had a friend who needed healing, and two

healers determined that he was touched by evil and sent him away. Actually, he reflected their own fear, and instead of using it as an opportunity to advance their souls, they fed their egos. We must not get stuck by limiting our growth. We have a responsibility to use all circumstances to heal ourselves and others.

4. **Law of *physician, heal thyself*:** See everything as an opportunity for personal growth, even if it brings discomfort and struggle. We know that we are loved and supported at all times by Source. Prayer works, and we are never alone. We must call on the angels frequently and often and refrain from believing that our power is generated by ourselves. Our power is generated through us. We are only channels. The true power comes from Higher Source. We must remember that we cannot transmit what we do not have, so we should continue to advance our souls' journeys at every opportunity.

5. **Law of being a clear channel:** Keep your energy elevated. Daily meditation and prayer are necessities. It is our responsibility to keep our frequencies clear and radiant. We must cease blaming others for our downfalls; learn protection prayers; and know that there are no bad people, only unfavorable behaviors, and behaviors can be changed. People and animals will be affected by our energy, and the pure essence of our presence can shift an entire group's energy field.

6. **Law of gratitude:** Say, "Thank you," to Higher Source for the opportunity to be of service, and thank your guides and angels. Thank the people and animals you assist for

the moments that allowed your personal growth, and most of all, thank yourself for being available to connect with your higher self.

CHAPTER 14

Protection

Imagination is creative energy inspired by the genius mind.

Many healers and psychics are under the impression that they are naturally protected just by maintaining high energy levels. Keeping our energy elevated is of utmost importance because it serves to keep us balanced and attracts people, places, and circumstances that are resonating on the same frequency levels.

However, high energy levels do not always protect us from intentional outside influences caused by dark, negative, karmic, or psychic attacks. In the event that these unfortunate circumstances take place, we need to use our own divine intention of white, gold, or violet light by calling on our protector guides and angels for assistance.

You might ask yourself, "Who would be sending me negative energy?"

There are entities that serve the darkness and are devoted to their cause just as there are entities that are light keepers serving to bring love and light into the world. The beings that serve the dark will send energy to block our light, and we may not be aware of these occurrences. They often use unconscious people to deliver negative situations to us in order to unbalance and bring our energy down, but the point is that we can do something about it with awareness and action.

There are many forms of protection that we can use to ensure the integrity of our light energy. Protection is a conscious action we take in addition to the maintenance of our energy centers and raising our vibrations.

The most common techniques that I teach are shielding and cord cutting.

> The vibration of light is the highest vibration (water being second). The higher we vibrate, the closer we are to light vibration.

Guardian Angels

Before we are conceived, we are assigned guardian angels to protect, guide, and unconditionally love us. They are always with us and never leave our sides. Because earth is a freewill plane, all angels need our permission to intervene in our earthly affairs. They will not intercede without our consent, but once we ask, they will always respond to every request for the highest good of all involved and according to our souls' intentions. They are symbiotic relationships because every time they serve us, they evolve through their tremendous love and devotion.

Each one of us has a celestial support team made up of archangels, ascended masters, spirit guides, deceased loved ones, and more. All these companions hear our prayers through an invisible communication network that connects us with all beings. They enhance our lives in numerable ways, including achieving clarity, goals, teaching, protection, and healing. When we pray, many appeal to our Creator, and when calling on specific angelic beings, we are asking for the Creator's appointed authorities and volunteers to assist directly through their specific talents bestowed on them by Source as advocates on our behalf to answer our requests.

I have listed archangels and Egyptian gods and goddesses, as well as their attributes. I urge you to call on these beings of light whenever you feel compelled and want assistance in your everyday life. It is important to know that part of liberation is asking for guidance and protection.

When I invoke guidance from the other realms, I keep my options open. I do not believe we need to know the specific names of angels and guides in order to ask and receive their assistance, but I do invite their guidance into my life with an open mind and heart and clear intentions.

Protection prayers need to be administered on a daily basis and sometimes on a situational basis. It is recommended that we shield our energy every twelve hours. Archangel Michael and his army of protection angels are the most common and effective helpers that unblock dark energy and deliver us from any harm. Archangel Michael showers us with sapphire-blue light that wraps around us like a butterfly cocoon.

Egyptian Gods and Goddesses

The Egyptian religion is complex and fascinating. I have included a list of Egyptian deities that are known for their protective and healing powers. Egyptian gods and goddesses represent aspects of nature, including animals and other portrayed mythological creatures. The ancient Egyptians were a polytheistic people who believed that gods and goddesses controlled the forces of the human, natural, and supernatural worlds. They believed in immortality, eternal life, and the afterlife. Their attitude toward death was deeply influenced through their belief in immortality. They regarded death as just a temporary interruption rather the cessation of life. To ensure the continuity of life after death, they paid homage to the gods and goddesses, both during and after their lives on earth. I like to think of the Egyptian gods and goddesses as principles that exist within us.

Protection Prayers and Meditations

My invocation goes like this: "I call on my I Am presence, the I Am presence of all humankind, Mother/Father God, the entire angelic realm, archangels, Metatron, ascended masters, all beings seen and unseen serving the divine love, light, beauty, power, grace, and truth of Higher Source to be with me right here and now. I ask that you guide, guard, and protect me until all are holy, ascended in the light, and free."

Shielding with White Light

Because we are spiritual, sensitive, and vibrational beings, we absorb energy, and sometimes this includes negativity and lower energies not intentionally transmitted by others. This is especially true if we are in a location or attend a gathering where lower unconscious vibrations occur or are present. People who are empathic or who easily osmose energy from others or even a location must learn to be aware of how to conserve their light.

As our receptivity to the spiritual realms increases, our sensitivity to negativity magnifies, and because of this, all light workers, empaths, spiritual seekers, and energy workers are perfect candidates to master the valuable tool of shielding. *Shielding* means using our intentions through imagination, visualization, and emotion to completely enclose ourselves within an orb or cocoon of sacred divine light.

It only takes a few moments to shield with light. Simply visualize yourself entirely surrounded in crystalline white light. Use your breath, and on the inhale, bring the light down through your crown chakra. On the exhale, extend the light out six feet (more or less) and seal it with golden light. You can invoke a light shield by saying, "Angels shield me in divine light *now!*"

These light shields will protect your loved ones, homes, offices,vehicles, and so forth. Make shielding a part of your daily ritual by using it first thing in the morning and before you go to sleep at night. There really is no wrong way to do this amazing incantation. We are powerful beings, and when we use our intentions by calling on our spirit guides and angels to bring forth divine light, it is done!

This light is loving, pure Divine Energy that is high vibrational and conscious energy. It protects and illuminates us simultaneously by its very nature. It cannot be misused by dark forces and will naturally repel any lower beings vibrating at a low frequency.

White Light

We can use any color from the rainbow to energize our energy fields, but white light is the standard protective light because it is incredibly powerful and effective. It automatically attracts the presence of the angelic realm and protects and uplifts our spirits.

White-Light Boundaries

This is essential for empathic people. This allows us to be in groups of people and keeps us protected while shifting a negative environment into a positive one.

Visualize: Pull white light from the great central sun, and allow it to pour down through your crown chakra and into your heart. Expand and send the white light out from your heart, and extend it around you in a continuous flow. You can direct this light toward a person whom you feel is not resonating in positive energy. Keep the current of light constantly flowing down from your crown chakra and out your heart while directing it to go wherever it is needed. Watch the energy shift in the person you are sending it to and even the environment around you.

This exercise becomes a natural routine after a while, just like breathing air. You will soon do this automatically whenever you enter unfamiliar territory or are surrounded by several people. You will not be able to absorb negative energy if you are continuously sending positive energy out.

Light Protection—Visualize

Imagine a huge ball of white light and loving energy hovering above your head. Take three deep cleansing breaths. With each breath, invite this light or energy to expand down through your body and into your heart.

Inhale the white light into your heart, and exhale the light from your heart, sending it out to surround you about twelve feet in every direction. Seal it with golden light, and release the exercise.

This should take only a couple of minutes, preferably in the morning before you start your day and at night before falling asleep. This is also a good protection when entering a group of people.

Cord Cutting

What Is a Psychic Cord?

Psychic cords are energetic bonds that form and develop between people. This occurs through sharing an emotional and intimate bond while in a relationship, especially when one partner is codependent and reliant, leading to an abusive entanglement. The patterns and beliefs that create these cords come from unsatisfied needs and deep emotional impressions. People involved in narcissistic relationships, whether from childhood or a romantic relationship (or both), go through life attracting the same liaisons.

Psychic cords are caused by many circumstances and often through emotionally traumatic events. Often, the cords occur as a result of allowing our boundaries to be disregarded—or, worse, not knowing how to establish boundaries in the first place. The problems that these cords create can be severe and affect us on emotional, subconscious, spiritual, energetic, and physical levels. They are the manifestations of blocked creative energy; repressed self-expression; loss of personal power; lack of self-esteem; unresolved anger, fear, resentment, dis-ease, or grief; weak or absent interpersonal boundaries; and depression.

The symptoms of cords will vary, but typically, a person will feel drained from the relationship when the cord is active. Letting go of an unhealthy relationship that includes a psychic cord can be difficult because the person we are leaving will still have a bond to us. Cutting a psychic cord eliminates the dark, negative, karmic, unconscious energy attached or sent to us by outside elements.

Say the following cord-cutting invocation aloud:

I invoke Archangel Michael and his army of protection angels to send me their sapphire-blue protection frequency flame to burn in, through, and around me, igniting my body, heart, mind, and spirit.

I ask that you wield your mighty swords [visualize lightning swords cutting the cords as you recite this] and sever all psychic, karmic, dark, or negative energy and any energy not serving the light attached or around me. Sever these cords in front, behind, above, below, to the right, and to the left of me. I ask that these energies be cut and returned back to their senders, multiplied by tens of thousands with love, light and grace ... right here and now. I ask that this process continue until all are holy, ascended in the light, and free! Beloved I Am, beloved I Am, beloved I Am!

Archangels and Egyptian Gods and Goddesses

The spirit realm holds a variety of helpers, and by special appointment from Source, they are tasked with helping humanity as we journey through our lives here on earth. They have the monumental charge of governing creation, including our soul contracts, life paths, life purpose, spiritual evolution, and the order of the natural world. They all have specific areas of expertise that qualify them to be called on at any time for assistance. They do not tire, because they can be in more than one place at one time. They ask us to call on them because when we acknowledge their presence and witness their miracles, we attribute their loving assistance with the hand of Source.

The list that follows includes some of the more well-known archangels and Egyptian gods and goddesses, including brief explanations of their areas of expertise and guidance.

Amon-Ra, "the Hidden One": He is the Egyptian god of the sun and air. He helps with fertility and our creative powers. He guides us toward our divine light and radiant force within. We can call on him when we need inspiration to complete a project or when we need to tap into our creative imaginations for ideas. He guides us inward toward self-realization and awareness and sustains the life of our planet, including animals, elementals, and seasons. Use citrine to connect with him.

Anubis, "God of the Afterlife": He is the Egyptian god who helps souls transition from life to death and assists our spirits in the afterlife. He is known for his strength, vitality, stamina, and protection from harm. We can call on him to protect our loved ones during transition and to help us emotionally cope through the process of our loss. Use carnelian crystal to connect with him.

Archangel Ariel, "Lion of God": She (sometimes seen in male form) is the guardian of nature. She defends, preserves, and supports the animal kingdom and commands the elemental spirits, including the undines/water, sylphs/air, salamanders/fire, and gnomes/earth. She teaches humans how to connect and heal through the properties of nature. Use rainbow tourmaline to increase contact with her.

Archangel Azrael, "Angel of God": He is the angel of transition. His enormous healing heart and light help people move through the depths of grief caused by loss. This could be from the death of a loved one, heartbreak from a relationship, job, loss, or discouragement over a dream. He alleviates the fear of those who are ready to cross over to the other side and helps prepare them for their journeys home. Use yellow calcite to reinforce connection and contact with him.

Bast, "Goddess of the Rising Sun": This Egyptian goddess protects families and individuals from illness, evil spirits, and disease and is associated with fertility, pregnancy, firefighters, and household cats. She is known to inspire music, dance, joy, and sensuality and help us with abundance and prosperity. She is a guardian of love and ancient wisdom. Use tiger eye stones to connect with her.

Archangel Chamuel, "One Who Sees God": He understands relationships and helps us discover a stronger love for ourselves by helping us find ways to forgive the past and build hope for the future.Through loving ourselves more deeply, we are able to form healthy relationships in love, work, and friendship and even strengthen our spiritual directives. He inspires us to find new ways to discover the beauty in ourselves so we can attract loving partnerships into our lives. Use red jasper to strengthen contact with him.

Gabriel, "Messenger": He (sometimes seen in female form) helps us to understand the meaning of our intuition and encourages us to act on behalf of divine guidance. He oversees forms of communication and inspires writers, artists, spokespeople, and performers to follow their creative dreams and helps us to deliver messages that will influence others to believe in the higher realms. Use aquamarine to increase connection with him.

Geb, "Hereditary Chief": The Egyptian god of vegetation helps people who are interested in learning the holistic healing arts of plant medicine. He is strongly related to the earth and assists farmers with the protection of their crops. He is known to help people discover healing remedies and find cures through intuitive thought and ideas. When we need grounding, we can call on him for support. Use obsidian to connect with his powers.

Hathor, "Lady of the Stars": This Egyptian goddess fosters fertility, pregnancy, childbirth, and motherhood. She encourages love, beauty, music, dancing, and exotic pleasure. She can be called on to help in romance and relationships. If you need encouragement to become more sensual, she will assist in teaching the arts of fragrance and various forms of beauty enhancements. Use malachite to strengthen connection with her.

Horus, "The One Far Above": This Egyptian god is known for the Eye of Horus, representing protection and prosperity. This symbol also represents self-realization within the six spiritual senses: (1) smell, (1) sight, (3) thought, (4) hearing, (5) taste, and (6) touch. He is called on for a deeper understanding of the insights connecting our anatomies to our spiritual purposes. He assists us in opening up the third eye to greater truths and wisdom. Use gold to connect with him.

Isis, "Queen of the Throne": This powerful Egyptian goddess is adored for her powers of protection and healing. She guides individuals through their creative processes and offers her magic healing properties toward regeneration and the resurrection of our higher selves. She offers the power of life and immortality to all who call on her and helps with redemption. If you need help with revelation and wisdom, she will guide you. She is known as the queen of the universe and the embodiment of cosmic order. Call on her for favorable outcomes in difficult situations of cosmic order. Use lapis lazuli to connect with her.

Archangel Jeremiel, "God's Mercy": He visits us through visions, dreams, and psychic awareness to communicate important messages. If we are seeking direction, purpose, or problem solving, or just need encouragement, he will guide us through our higher minds. He gives us hope, inspiration, and ideas for how we can improve our lives. Use amethyst to make a stronger connection with him.

Archangel Jophiel, "Divine Beauty": This Egyptian god can help us organize our thoughts and aid in clear thinking when we feel overwhelmed or unsure about something. He can help us tap into our true potential and uncover our unique gifts and talents. We can call on him if we need inspiration or a creative idea to enhance a project. Use smokey quartz to form a strong connection with him.

Metatron, "Angel of Empowerment": He helps us access our intuitive abilities to strengthen our higher senses. He assists us in letting go of everything that no longer serves us through intense light work and aura cleansing. He encourages us to use healing methods to raise our vibrations to allow for more clarity, direction, and service. We can call on him to help us align our energy centers and raise our awareness. Metatron uses the number frequencies of 11:11 as a portal to get our attention and awaken our true spiritual paths, purposes, and destinies. Use sardonyx to strengthen connection with him.

Archangel Michael, "Who Is like God": He is the protector, defender of the light, and bringer of truth and justice. He is called on to help guide us out of fear, doubt, and disappointment and aid us when we are facing troubling times. He has an army of soldiers by his side that free us from the holds of anything that is not serving the light, and he provides us with protection, guidance, healing, and clarity. He can help us release negativity and bring us the courage and strength we need to balance our lives. He also assists us with abundance and prosperity. Use golden topaz to form a close connection with him.

Osiris, "Lord of Silence": This Egyptian god helps guide people through personal transformation. If you are studying to be a shaman, priest, or priestess, he can help you to learn the alchemy of energy. He helps us understand the value of the elements in nature and how to use our energy to protect ourselves by becoming strong and resistant to harm and to gain stamina. He guides individuals through the process of rebirth and renewal. Use red jasper to work with him.

Archangel Raguel, "Friend of God": He is concerned with justice and helps people find ways to fight for others who are oppressed or neglected. He motivates us to support worthy causes that benefit the less fortunate. He encourages us to find order out of chaos and resolve conflicts through understanding, fairness, compassion, and peace. He teaches us how to focus our anger at injustice in constructive ways. He will bring healing and harmony to situations of misunderstandings. Use aquamarine to connect closer to him.

Archangel Raphael, "Angel of Healing": He helps us through the healing process concerning our minds, bodies, hearts, and spirits so we can find ultimate health and help others find peace. He guides our intuition so we can make the right decisions concerning our care or the care of our loved ones. He transmutes anything that is blocking us from our recovery and quickens the healing process. He is also concerned with our environment and encourages us to be stewards of our planet. He will show us how to use our powers of influence to beautify nature in creative ways. Use emerald to connect closely with him.

Archangel Raziel, "Keeper of Secrets": He guides people to discover the meaning within the sacred mysteries. He encourages us to heighten our psychic abilities and use our powers of clairvoyance, clairaudience, clairsentience, and claircognizance. One of the ways he assists us is through uncovering the ancient wisdom that has been hidden for centuries. He helps us use our imagination and bring our dreams into fruition. He supports our efforts to tap into our spiritual insights and encourages us to move forward to fulfill our life missions. Use clear quartz to connect with him.

Sandalphon, "Brother": He helps people identify their unique talents and potential while developing these gifts to fulfill their life missions. He guides us to connecting with the Divine by balancing our earth energies with our spiritual devotions. He works with Metatron in strengthening our prayers and intentions to work with the light and achieve the greatest-possible outcomes stemming from our inner dreams and visions. Use turquoise to connect with him.

Sekhmet, "She Who Is Powerful": This Egyptian goddess is associated with medicine and healing. She is called on to cure the sick and terminally ill. She is a patron for nurses and physicians. If there is a plague or disease for which doctors have not found a cure, she is the one to call on for assistance. She works with individuals to gain personal empowerment. Use Kalahari jasper to work with her.

Seth, "Pillar of Stability": This Egyptian god protects travelers and foreigners on their journeys away from home. If you are lost and not sure what path to take, he will help you find your way to safety. He is also called on during violent storms, earthquakes, and tornadoes to guide you to security. He is strong and powerful and uses his abilities to protect those who appear to have strayed. He is helpful when you need motivation to take action because he represents movement. Use carnelian to work with him.

Thoth, "He Who Is like the Ibis": This Egyptian god helps those who are involved with writing, research, interpretation, ancient wisdom, mathematics, magic, language, science, bookkeeping, and withholding the law. If we need assistance with problem solving, he will help us weigh the pros and cons before coming to a conclusion. He is credited for inventing the calendar and controlling space and time. Use the emerald to connect with him.

Archangel Uriel, "God Is My Light": He guides us toward divine wisdom when we need help with learning, problem solving, decision making, and releasing destructive behavior or emotions that prevent us from seeking the truth. When we are confused, he illuminates our minds with clarity and confidence. He warns or deter us from harmful situations and guide us in the right direction. He often uses inspiration in the form of creative ideas or innovative thinking to move us into action. Use citrine to connect with him.

Archangel Zadkiel, "Righteousness of God": He inspires us to use forgiveness and mercy when healing from painful events in our lives, whether they simply happened to us or occurred as a result of our actions. He helps us remove unhealthy living circumstances from our lives and focus on positive solutions to our problems. He encourages us to behold our divine essence and move toward faith and compassion when situations appear dark and hopeless. He works with the alchemy of the violet flame to heal generations of trauma and imbalance within our energy fields. Use amethyst to work with him.

A Powerful Protection Exercise For Beginner Light Workers

Visualize and invoke a waterfall of light rinsing around your entire being, washing away anxiety, stress, tension, and negativity. Allow your inner light and authenticity to shine through. Grant this light permission to fill your heart, and let it expand.

As the light expands outward, your throat chakra opens. This is your clairaudient center and the source of your ability to speak your truth and to hear messages from your angels and guides. Let your heart light continue to expand, activating your third eye (your clairvoyant sight) and your ability to see through the veils of the illusion.

Continue to expand this glorious light, opening your crown chakra and your direct link to the portal of the Divine. This allows you to ground divine light into the present moment. Now step into being a pillar on the earth, radiating forth your entire embodiment of light, and drawing in light from above, allow it to expand around and through the human heart grid, out into the crystalline grid, and across the entire planet. You are literally creating and vibrating waves of positive energy out and beyond you.

Endure this expansion of crystalline light, Source presence, and the full multidimensional light of your soul, which includes many higher selves, higher beings, skills, abilities, and an infinite supply of love—all accessed by going inward.

PART III

<u>CHAPTER 15</u>

PTSD—Portal to Spiritual Doorways

I believe I am here for a reason and my purpose is Greater than my
challenges
—Rumi

I suffered from PTSD most of my life, and I am going to speak of the benefits derived from my PTSD experience. Anyone who has reason to experience the ramifications of this disorder will attest to the fact that there are little to no benefits acquired from having it. I can verify that, until recently, I never considered a positive perspective to evolve out of my nervous disorder.

PTSD is a condition experienced by people who have undergone military combat, sexual violence, physical assault, childhood abuse, accidents, torture, environmental disasters (e.g., fires, earthquakes, tornadoes, flash floods), or life-altering experiences (e.g., the death of a loved one). It is not limited to the preceding occurrences; any event that causes individuals to fear for their personal lives and well-being can fall under this category.

I lived with PTSD for thirty years following two major traumatic events that happened within three months of each other, and at the time of these experiences, I not only feared for my life but disassociated physically, emotionally, and mentally from my body at the time the crises took place. Because I was not 100 percent present during these attacks, it took decades of therapy and medication to guide me through the remembering process and back to recovery.

I was twelve years old when I was abducted by racial gang members, raped, and dropped off in the middle of the night in backcountry orchards. I was later threatened at knifepoint that if I ever reported this abduction to anyone, not only would I be killed, but my family would as well. After being stalked and threatened with other unspeakable actions, I had every reason to believe that the threats to me and my family members' lives were sincere. I lived in a constant state of terror, fear, and insomnia and developed an unhealthy emotional dependency on others for many years. I tried to hide and forget these horrors by storing them deep within my subconscious with the use of alcohol and street drugs. This worked for a long time—until it stopped working, and I eventually had to seek outside help to find a level of comfort that I could live with. I realized that I was never addicted to just one thing. I was addicted to filling a void within myself with everything other than my own love.

What I learned about my PTSD is that it affected my nervous system and made me hypervigilant, and I developed a keen sense of awareness for the environment around me. Nicotine, sugar, and caffeine only aggravated and perpetuated my condition. These ingredients are harmful to a person suffering from an elevated nervous system. I also developed asthma and chronic bronchitis because of my untreated illness. I realized that my condition altered my endocrine system, which is the collection of several glands, including the pineal, pituitary, pancreas, ovaries, thyroid, parathyroid hypothalamus, and adrenal. This made sense to me because I suffered from insomnia, nightmares, anxiety, and depression, and I had the beginning symptoms of autoimmune disease. I knew that my nervous system was heightened, but I was not prepared to endure the long-term effects that this would have on me.

It was brought to my awareness that not all the symptoms of PTSD are negative. I was aware that this state of hyper-alertness was serving me by opening psychic portals that would not have been available to me otherwise. At the time of my traumatic experiences, I disassociated from my body, and when I asked myself, "Where did I go?" I remember looking down at the situation and, at that moment, knowing I was safe and out of harm's way. I believe I escaped through an etheric portal, and this is how I discovered the existence of doorways and their potential to serve, protect, and save my life.

This portal, once opened, never closed. After these occurrences, whenever I found myself in uncomfortable circumstances, I would revisit this portal, or disassociate, as they say. I had to go to therapy to learn how to be in my body in present time and master how to trust and feel safe again. Once I began healing the trauma, I accessed the portal and entered these doorways of spiritual survival during meditation. I found a warmth and comfort that only a person with PTSD or who has faced a near-death experience could ever appreciate. Fear of the unknown was secondary to the trauma that overtook my life for many years. I began visiting with spirits from the other side because I believe this portal or doorway lifted the veils that separated me from the other realms.

I credit this process to my pineal, pituitary, and hypothalamus glands being activated by the cause of my PTSD.

People who have experienced a traumatic situation naturally exit into an unnatural realm and open a psychic door to the unknown. At the time, it is frightening, dark, and often indescribable. We are not sure how we got there, but once opened, the door becomes available to us at any time. Many victims return to this realm only to revisit the trauma, and others get lost in the darkness, not knowing how to free themselves.

Because the portal is originally opened during a crisis, it is common to believe that this is where the trauma lives—but not necessarily. Once we understand that we opened a door to another realm, and if we are fortunate enough to heal the trauma, we can visit the realm under alternate circumstances. This doorway can lead to more positive aspects of the unknown, but very few get this far. All of us who have experienced a deep level of trauma know that we are different. We know we have been places that others have never dreamed possible. We exist with a level of understanding that does not seem useful in the material or spiritual world. But it is.

There are things about me that have changed because of my challenging experience. I became more susceptible to spiritual guidance and available to psychic awareness. When I healed the wound of my past, I discovered the opening to the unknown. I began to examine this portal that had once haunted me and allowed it to become an integral part of my life. I was afraid of it at first, but when I began to channel my energy toward these spiritual doorways, the negative physical, emotional, and mental symptoms that I had been living with subsided. The autoimmune-disease symptoms brought on from the overuse of my nervous system had all but disappeared. I began to meditate, pray, exercise, and journal daily. Although I admit it has taken time to add these qualities into my routine, this guidance has been crucial to solving the problems that I suffered with for many years.

As I mentioned before, I used street drugs and alcohol to escape from the repeating memories haunting my psyche. After many years of abusing these ingredients, I became addicted. When I was tired of running from my demons, I entered a recovery program and allowed the twelve steps of recovery to nurture me back into the world of reality. I believe that everything happens for a reason and that my addictions were a part of my soul-life purpose. Where else could I get clean and sober, receive spiritual counsel, learn twelve steps to live by, and benefit from a fellowship of people who supported my efforts? Without this guidance, I would never have had the courage to enter the spiritual doorways available to me. Becoming a spiritual warrior is not about just being available for spiritual guidance; it is having the willingness to take the right action in the face of fear.

I acknowledge that the path of the wounded healer involves traumatic experiences for many of us. We are meant to experience the unforgivable to overcome and heal ourselves so we can build a guiding bridge for others to follow. We come into this lifetime and take on difficult assignments in hopes of gaining the courage and wisdom of the mystic masters. If we survive, we become examples of spiritual warriors and share our experiences, strength, and hope with those who carry the same or similar fates.

Could it be that PTSD stands for the *portal to spiritual doorways* instead of *posttraumatic stress disorder?* Could our endocrine systems be altered during traumatic experiences to help us survive these circumstances of darkness and alter the very glands that affect our inner sight, visions, and intuition?

Could this twist of fate be a beacon of light that triggers our awareness and leads us into doorways of spiritual truth?

It has been my experience that I have just begun to enter the outer layers of this discovery and all it has to offer. The hypervigilance that once haunted me is now my guiding light. I am grateful for the sensitivities I feel because of my once frightening experience. I am open to the awareness of my constructive manner. I am walking through psychic portals and learning ancient wisdom in other realms. I am learning to trust my intuition on a deeper level and follow through with my instincts. Instead of insomnia and nightmares, I have dreams and premonitions. I no longer believe I suffer from PTSD; rather, I have earned the power to travel through spiritual doorways.

CHAPTER 16

The Awakening

Awakening is the moment we open our minds and hearts to the one true Source and original creator of our souls. This portal allows for a new level of light to encompass our beings so that we begin to perceive and experience a deeper understanding of what life really is in the contrast of shadows and light.

Spiritual awakening is an initiation process of fully activating our view of reality through an enlightened landscape. An awakened state is one in which we are united to our higher selves and higher consciousness and the present moment with awareness.

It is the juncture where we drop our stories, past conditioning, and limiting beliefs and explore firsthand the answer to the question, Who am I?

It is a moment of transcendence, and in this realization, it stretches across, touching all areas of our lives.

Awakening spiritually alters the way we move through the world, beckoning an inner sense of peace and serenity to govern our actions and reactions.

An awakening can be gradual, or it can strike by lightning when one single event releases a flood of insights, changing our awareness of reality completely. There really is no set definition as to how an awakening should occur; people experience it differently and in their own unique ways.

A spiritual awakening is an ongoing, ever-flowing, and unfolding process. It is not a onetime occasion, and just like waking up in the morning in physical life, it is something we are aware of every day. It is the process of fully remembering who we are as conscious ethical beings as we travel along our divinely guided paths. We turn away from layers of illusions present in the physical world and choose to become aware of who we really are and what we know as our own inner truths.

The process can be demanding with regard to our mental, emotional, and physical well-being. Depending on our conditioning, it can cause cognitive dissonance, resulting in mental conflict with ourselves. It may immobilize us for a period of time, and patience is required to process all this newly acquired information. We need to find ways to integrate all that we have learned. An awakening is not an ephemera; we do not just walk away from it unaffected.

As the saying by Oliver Wendell Holmes goes, "Once a mind has been stretched by a new experience, it can never go back to its old dimensions."

Acquiring new insights and shifting into new paradigms often contradict societal conditioning, and this takes time to integrate. We have to find ways to cope with the understanding of the true nature of reality even though it is incompatible with what society expects from us. After awakening and tasting enlightenment, we reintegrate back into society slowly because our new awareness has shifted into a higher state of consciousness, and we need to find new ways of being in the world. We need time to stabilize our energy after an awakening.

This stage requires us to unravel years of conditioning and modify the structures of our minds. Everything in our lives shifts as a result of our choosing to live more truthfully. After an awakening, many people pick up their lives exactly where they left off and integrate the newly gathered knowledge, wisdom, and insights. For others, this process introduces and engages a new quest that changes their lives completely.

It is not that it requires effort, work, or practice. Spiritual awakening is available to anyone ready to let go of false beliefs—whether it takes years or one impactful moment. We are required to stabilize this transcendence and repeatedly return to presence, quiet our minds, and tune in to our heart centers.

Before we begin to wake up, life is a series of coincidences or events that we have a hand in orchestrating. It appears as though life is something we can even exert our will on to influence and make things happen.

It is often difficult to understand that everything happening in life unfolds perfectly as it should because our tendency is to believe that bad things happened to us and good things happened because of us.

But when we awake, applying presence to our lives and universal experience as human beings, we begin to understand and feel a positive flow to life.

Our presence allows us to relax, recognizing that we are always tapped into the Divine Energy of the universe; our coincidences stop feeling random; and our intuitions become stronger.

A spiritual awakening is not designed to be a challenging time in our lives. Incredibly painful catalysts, like dark nights of the soul, can lead to a spiritual awakening, and being attached to illusions of cultural dreams as they dissolve provides the means for challenges related to an awakening process. But these are not really symptoms of a spiritual awakening—more symptoms of struggling to surrender the illusions rather than going with the flow. This is where people run into difficulty in the awakening process.

One person at a time, humanity is now undergoing the spiritual- awakening process. Individuals across the planet are waking up and letting go of their minds' grip on illusion to experience profound changes in consciousness and accept expanded perspectives.

The awakening process involves realizing from deep within and all around us that the separation, limitation, beliefs, and models for success and happiness in the physical world are rooted in deception.

It is a highly personal process that is deeply challenging as the very foundations we have built for how to live and succeed in the world start to crumble away. Awakening will reveal the many matrix programs of society and how they weigh us down and hide us from our true nature, light, and infinite potential.

Without awakening, we risk staying on the path of the external by pursuing the unfulfilling markers of success and happiness dictated by society, like money; material success; fame; power; the "good job"; or the deep-seated happiness myth of buying a home, getting married, having kids, and living happily ever after. Through awakening, we see through the illusions of the physical world and recognize that nothing external ever brings us true fulfillment, success, and happiness.

Once we are awakened, these external markers present themselves as a result of finding and following our soul-life agreements, but in and of themselves, they are only by-products of right living. Awakening itself is a shift in consciousness, and from this new perspective, everything else in reality begins to shift around us as well, and we realize we live in a world of impermanence.

Spiritual awakening can be effortless as we let go of layers of illusion and move toward authenticity, integrity, unconditional love, and truth.

It is a beautiful and powerful epiphany taking the first steps down a path of infinite possibility. At this juncture, we must make a choice: Do we choose to serve only ourselves, or do we serve and love others, recognizing our connection and the Divine in all?

Yes, we all have free will, and there are many opportunities for us to choose and create within our life experiences. With every choice, point, or decision in life, a fork in the road is created where new opportunities, options, and decisions are revealed. While our choices lead to certain experiences and outcomes in life, all the possibilities we encounter ultimately lead us toward whatever will serve in alignment with our soul-life contracts, our true reason and purpose for being alive in this incarnation.

The reality of our nature awakens the truth that we are far more than physical beings. We are multidimensional spiritual beings, and prior to our present lives, we agreed to limit our awareness of this, to be fully immersed in duality, separation, and illusion. If we are going through an awakening, then we also agreed to set the stage for ourselves to have the experience of waking up and remembering this truth.

In other words, it is our souls that trigger our awakening process. There were several events, books, people, experiences, and even movies that played a role in our pre–awakening process, and all our life experiences have essentially been preparing us for the journey of dissolving the veils of illusion, rinsing sleep away from our eyes, reclaiming our power as cocreators in the physical world, and being fully awakened divine beings.

The signs of a spiritual awakening are different for everyone. Awakening is a magnificent and magical time, though some are challenged by knowing the truth and not wanting to let go of the illusion.

Awakening spiritually is commonly not an easy path, but it is filled with blessings, magic, and opportunities to live with greater love, joy, passion, and fulfillment than ever before. It is a turning point in our lives as we align with the knowing of our highest purpose and bring ourselves into alignment with it.

It only happens one step at a time. We must be gentle with ourselves, honor our presence, stay positive about where we are headed, and, when in doubt, sit still, quiet our minds, open our hearts, and connect with our angels and guides, because they will help us access the brilliant light and wisdom we carry within. Be filled with the knowing that everything is happening as it should.

Signs of a Spiritual Awakening
1. You crave more solitude.
2. You see through the illusions created by society.
3. Synchronicity and repeating numbers happen more frequently.
4. You desire meaning and purpose for your life.
5. You feel completely alone, lost, or misplaced.
6. New opportunities, relationships and abundance show up, seemingly out of nowhere.
7. You experience a change in sleep patterns.
8. You begin to experience periods of "manifestation on demand," miracles, and super flow as you experience your new vibration.

9. You hear ringing in your ears.
10. The world around you feels different as if you've stepped into a new reality.

<u>CHAPTER 17</u>

The Ascension

The ancient Egyptians believed in the personal ascension long before Christ came to remind us of our human purpose here on earth.

The Egyptians used symbols as a way to communicate and tap into the archetypal mind. These symbols represent the ascension process in terms of eternal life, rebirth, and the afterlife. The ancient Egyptian symbols include the ankh, representing life and immortality; ouroboros, representing rebirth, re-creation of life, and perpetuity; scarab, representing the sun, re-creation of life, resurrection, and transformation; tree of life, representing eternal life and knowledge of the cycles of times; and the Menat, representing life, fertility, birth, rebirth, potency, and joy.

Egyptian numerology is a form of ancient wisdom, pointing the way toward personal ascension and spiritual freedom. It helps us raise awareness and the energy frequencies necessary for our souls' evolution. Numbers are symbols that carry vibrations and special meaning to those who resonate on a higher-level consciousness.

I have believed in personal attainment and ascension most of my life. Along my journey, there were three distinct occurrences that aligned themselves, allowing me the opportunity to discover this phenomenon at quite a young age.

Being brought up in the Catholic religion, I was introduced to the life path of Jesus. His resurrection and ascension intrigued me, and I often pondered the meaning behind His unique and powerful messages. I intuitively knew there was more to the story than just going to church on Sundays, reading the Bible, and not eating meat on Fridays.

The more I listened to His life adventures, I believed Jesus came to show us that we too could ascend, and the power behind worshiping Him as a human miracle worker stopped working for me. I did not believe that He'd come here to be worshipped. In fact, I felt it was ethically wrong to just honor Him as the Son of God because we are all sons and daughters of God. I knew He'd come to set a living example and that if I did not understand this, I was missing the whole point of my upbringing as a Catholic. The problem was that nobody else was sharing my point of view. Every devout Catholic who I knew was worshipping Him for all the wrong reasons. This frustrated me, and I started to lose interest in the religion business. I wanted more out of my spiritual experience, and I knew I was right, but how could all these other people be wrong? Out of self-preservation, I kept my findings to myself.

Meanwhile, as I began to sort out my revelations at the age of sixteen, I was introduced to the teachings of the ascended masters through the Summit Lighthouse University in Santa Barbara, California. This acquainted me to other ascended higher beings who had previously walked human lives, perfected alignment of their soul-life agreements, and no longer needed to incarnate to dissolve past karma. I learned that they have their own hierarchy in the spirit realm, just like we have our own form of government here on earth, and they work to help elevate the consciousness of humankind. I was fascinated by this concept because it calibrated with my Catholic epiphany. Some of these other masters were Saint Germain, Mother Mary, Paul the Venetian, Serapis Bey, Saint Germain, Paramahansa Yogananda, John the Baptist, Buddha, El Morya, Isis, Kuthumi, Lady Nada, and Master Hilarion.

At this university, I learned about chakras; how to increase my energy field and cleanse my aura through decrees, mantras, and affirmations; and more. I studied color healing and how to raise my vibration to connect with ascended masters in higher realms. I became fascinated with Eastern philosophy, reincarnation, astrology, numerology, palmistry, dream interpretations, nutrition, and psychic abilities. I started to call myself an *extended Catholic* because I rode the religion as far as it would take me and lifted the cathedral ceiling to explore further.

The most convincing component contributing to my awareness of the ascension happened prior to my introduction to the teachings of the ascended masters and came as a personal experience of the dark night of the soul. I was fourteen years old, suffering from deep depression and anxiety after my sexual assault. I became despondent and isolated and lost my desire to live. I was silently crying and praying to die every night before I went to sleep.

After weeks of enormous emotional pain, I awoke one morning, and a shift in consciousness occurred. This is the best way I can describe it. I did not physically die like I'd prayed for, but rather, the part of me that had been suffering died and ascended to a higher level, bringing me greater awareness and understanding regarding my current circumstances. I was no longer in pain but instead filled with a level of enlightenment, wisdom, and knowledge from a spiritual nature. I had an awakening—was changed—and I could not explain it. My life catapulted from that day on, and it taught me that there is more to life than what I can see with my eyes. I had an internal knowingness that I am here for a reason, and from that day forward, I believed in miracles.

Between my Catholic epiphany, the teachings of the ascended masters, and my personal awakening, all three of these experiences and revelations confirmed the belief that my purpose in life is to ascend from one dimension to the next, and if Jesus could do it, so can we. A personal ascension is shifting awareness, letting go of old paradigms, opening to the Divine, educating our egos, following our passions, trusting our intuition, elevating human love into divine love, and allowing grace to fill us with self-love, and all this is possible through a spiritual awakening.

In Egyptian numerology, it is possible to ascend from the frequencies we were born into. Following our soul-life paths, purposes, and destinies and adopting the specific initiations or virtues assigned to each number assist individuals to complete their life missions. Once we complete our missions, we ascend back to the great void, alpha and omega, the sacred drum of life, or the zero-point field.

All of us are made of light frequencies. In my previous book, I describe how, the moment we are born, we sound the drum of life, which determines the frequency of our soul-life journeys. Using this resonance frequency, we travel through life experiencing the world around us. The universe recognizes this vibration and, like a magnet, attracts to us people, places, things, events, and circumstances that echo with our nature. We take all our moments as a means to explore, entertain, expand, experience, and elevate.

We are meant to return to the drum of life exempt of sound or at higher frequencies. If we enter the drum, void, or zero-point field at the same or a lower frequency, we must return to earth again and again until we have vibrated high enough to dissolve or elevate our sound.

Understanding our dimensions gives us a clearer perspective of where we are in the cycle of life. I use the following descriptions to help my students grasp the multilayers of consciousness available for us to choose from.

I most certainly can identify with all three dimensions, and just to be clear, we can ascend higher than the fifth dimension.

CHAPTER 18

Emerging into the Miraculous World of the Fifth Dimension

When there are no leaders to follow, you must become one.

Egyptian numerology lies under the premise that before birth, we contracted with a karmic board in the spirit realm to achieve specific goals, complete karmic lessons, advance in our spiritual evolution, and understand our pure essence of being as divine love.

Because we are subjected to birth amnesia when incarnated, we encoded these vital lessons in our birth names and birth dates. When we begin to understand the powerful forces behind these frequencies, we open to this accurate mapping as it points to our soul-life missions, soul-life paths, purposes, and destinies within.

The paradigm for numbers has shifted over the past few decades, and it is vital we acknowledge this change and accept the ancient wisdom now available to us during these radical times of evolution.

Egyptian numerology takes our reflection and enhances the view by lifting these frequencies into the fifth dimension, showing us what is possible to achieve in this lifetime. The fifth dimension is described as the plane of love and living totally from the heart.

This gives us the opportunity to discover areas of our lives that have the greatest potential and what they look like in an elevated frequency rating. It is compatible with getting a new lens prescription in order tosee ourselves clearly.

If we are already living our highest frequencies, then this type of charting is used as a geographical confirmation that we are on the right track, or it can be used as a reference point for what is possible to achieve in a perspective not always revealing. It offers a description of what our lives look like when we live from our heart chakra. Most people do not have an idea that they can exceed the frequency that they are presently resonating with.

The guidelines that I have laid out in the following chapters are only examples of what we are meant to accomplish on our short visit here in this incarnation. It is important to briefly understand dimensions and the possibilities each one holds for us in order to determine if we are ready to excel on our soul-life journeys.

It is an undeniable fact that we have been emerging into the fifth dimension for quite some time now. Spiritual leaders have been talking about this evolution for decades, hence the movement into the Aquarian age. Prophets have been singing, writing, and speaking of this transformation through songs and literature like *The Celestine Prophecy*, *A Course of Miracles*, Kahlil Gibran's *The Prophet*, and John Lennon's "Imagine."

It is our nature to evolve. Ask the caterpillar that goes through the chrysalis process, transforming into a butterfly, or the mighty pine or oak tree that sprouts from a tiny seed that we can hold in the palms of our hands. We live in exciting times, and our moment has come to take flight into new dimensions. Before we commit to leaps and bounds into the unknown abyss of the fifth level of spiritual comfort, let us review our past relationship with the previous dimensions.

My goal is to not only assist souls through the process of this emergence but solidify our existence as spiritual beings and prepare for the spinning of even more greatness. We are emerging, unfolding, evolving, becoming, growing, being, moving, and developing all the time. It is our nature to do so. We resonate with the butterfly and the mighty oak more than we realize. Some of us are unraveling layers before we can become weightless enough to change. Years of hard- core conditioning calcifies our souls, and when we analyze our belief systems, let go of generations of old ideas and beliefs that no longer serve us, and open our minds, we begin to emerge into new possibilities again and again.

Third, Fourth, and Fifth Dimensions

According to ascension teachings, the earth and all beings living here are in the process of shifting into a whole new level of reality, where consciousness of love, compassion, peace, and spiritual wisdom prevails. This is called the *fifth dimension*. This shift will be complete within the next couple of decades, and individuals will move into the fifth dimension at their own rate as their frequencies elevate enough to resonate to the vibration of the higher dimensions. Many spiritual teachings state that the passage the earth and humanity are taking into the fifth dimension was planned for eons and started its ascent using December 21, 2012, as the midpoint shift, and it continues to excel and pick up speed as time goes on.

Dimensions are not places or locations but levels of consciousness that vibrate at an assured rate. There are numerous dimensions; the fourth and fifth are simply higher than the one we have been existing in. Ascension into even higher dimensions will continue after we have reached the tip of the fifth dimension, and each dimension vibrates at a higher rate than the one below. On the higher dimensions, there is a clearer, wider perspective of reality and a greater level of awareness, where we experience more freedom, divine love, greater power, and more opportunity to create reality. In order for a higher dimension to be available, we need to vibrate in resonance with it. Shifting from one level of consciousness to the next higher one means becoming established on it so that we do not get pulled back down to the previous one.

The fifth dimension relates to the status of heaven and is referred to as the *plane of light, nirvana,* and *love.* It is called the *miraculous world.* In this plane, fear, pain, isolation, and suffering do not exist, because we no longer suffer from any form of illusion or separation. We continuously experience the oneness of Mother/Father Creator, and if we incarnate from this dimension, we will be luminous light beings traveling by the application of divine will. We know we are in the fifth dimension when we

- experience the magnificent reality of living in faith that we are in the hands of Spirit at all times;
- perceive everything as permitted and impermanent, even if it is sometimes unpleasant, because we know that Spirit is directing our course;

- realize in many areas of our lives and especially our life purposes that the walls of time and space are not limitations;
- live with the understanding that when we remain open and empty simultaneously, the universe manifests miracles through us;
- observe that miracles are predominant;
- allow visions of heaven on earth;
- find that insights manifest naturally; and
- live in a state of gratitude and appreciation for all that is.

To enter the fifth dimension and stay there, you must check all mental and emotional baggage at the door because there is no fear, regret, anger, hostility, guilt, suffering, or sense of separation that exists there. Mastery over thought is a prerequisite, and manifestation on this plane is instantaneous. When we think about something, it materializes.

People communicate through telepathy and have the ability to read one another's thoughts and feelings with ease. The experience of time is described as everything happening simultaneously, with no distinctions between past, present, and future. Many of us have experiences or dreams that feel like visits to the fifth dimension, and these are exhilarating, exciting, and hopeful. They keep us motivated to follow through with difficulties that sometimes arise while traveling through the fourth dimension and into the fifth.

The third dimension is a state of consciousness that is extremely limited and restricted. Because we have been living in the third-dimensional reality for many lifetimes, we assume that this is the only reality available to us. We think this is how reality is, and we do not realize that, in general, it is a very narrow experience. The third-dimensional operating system runs on rigid beliefs, with an inflexible set of rules and confined limitations. For example, in the third dimension, we learn to accept that bodies are solid; they cannot merge with one another or walk-through walls. Everything is subject to gravity, physical objects do not disappear, and we cannot read another person's mind. There is a solid belief in duality where judgment and fear are pervasive.

Most people live somewhere between the third and fourth dimensions and only get a glimpse of the fifth dimension during their lifetimes. The third dimension is the plane of physical reality and conscious being. It is called the *material world*. This is where energy congeals into a dark, dense pool of matter. This is the plane of thought or mind, and the densest stratum of this plane contains our worldly and material thoughts. Because of our planetary coding or consciousness, we identify with matter and therefore become dense ourselves.

The universe allows the illusion of free will in the third and fourth dimensions, which gives us the experience of acting like saints, demons, or somewhere in between—and always by choice. Beings who believe that the third is the only dimension suffer from the illusion of separation from their spirits. The physical senses do not detect Spirit, which is beyond physical form, but if we are not one with Spirit, then we cannot be at one with others. Our ability to experience beauty and empathy while in such density shows that we do live in a loving universe, and if we have the ability to contact the higher strata of the mind world by training the corresponding parts of our brain, as all seekers have attempted to do, we will gain inconceivable knowledge. Some experiences belonging to the third dimension are

- being caught up in a stream of thought,
- planning sexual strategies,
- being sarcastic,
- being obnoxious,
- being critical,
- physically or verbally attacking someone,
- proving we are right or someone else is wrong, and
- defending or claiming our spaces.

The way that we perceive and define ourselves implies which world we are living in. We take a stand for the validity of the material world when we identify ourselves as being

- hard workers;
- smart people;
- honest people;
- business people;
- responsible people;
- funny people; and
- students, teachers, parents, spouses, or children.

The fourth dimension is the bridge most of us are on now and will continue on for a relatively short period of time. In traveling through the fourth dimension, we prepare ourselves for the elevator ride up to the fifth. Many of us have had experiences of the fourth dimension for a number of years without realizing it. We experience the fourth dimension when we have moments of a spiritual awakening and feelings of opening the heart. It can arise when we are feeling clear and quiet inside, everything within and around us feels lighter and less rigid, and there is a sense of spaciousness and tranquility that overcomes our entire beings. Time is no longer linear in the fourth dimension, and we take comfort in the present moment without interest or even awareness of past and future events. We discover that time is malleable and stretches and condenses, much to our third-dimensional surprise. We manifest desires faster and notice that something we think about will show up very quickly. In general, when we experience joy, love, and gratitude, we are allowing fourth-dimensional consciousness to surface.

The fourth dimension is the plane of truth, as well as the astral plane. It is called the *magical world*. This dimension is a gray polarized plane that houses forces of light and darkness. The battle between good and evil starts here. This is the plane where our will resides, and it is the dimension of the individual self, or ego. It is our egos that use the physical, astral, and mind bodies as tools to achieve their purpose. When mind, body, and spirit are completely aligned with divine will, in harmony and balanced, one with the other, we are omnipotent and have achieved the conquest over matter. After we train carefully, it is possible for us to leave the physical body safely in the nourishing care of its etheric web to go on a dimensional journey. This is called astral travel. Experiences belonging to the fourth dimension are as follows:

- magic
- time travels
- karma
- reincarnation
- luck
- psychic surgery
- out-of-body flight
- mind reading
- disembodied spirits

- enchantment
- astral travel

These are all sources of this plane. You are living in the magical world when you find yourself engaged in any of the following activities:

- being superstitious
- having sexual fantasies
- psychically attacking or defending someone
- fighting for a good or bad cause
- psychically manipulating another
- working out karma
- preaching
- using white or black magic

We are currently in what is called a transitional era, or the end of times. These are the moments we experience the death of third-dimensional reality and begin to travel through the new and unknown landscapes of the fourth dimension. In essence, one whole structure of existence is collapsing while a brand-new one is emerging. It is to be expected that some chaos, confusion, and disorientation will reign both within and around us as we adapt to a whole new way of experiencing reality. Many of us are beginning to experience radical changes in our lives as we enter into these stages. Whatever does not serve us any longer as we shift into a higher dimension has to fall away. This includes old relationships, lifetime careers, approaches to life we have traditionally taken for granted, outdated sense of identity, limited beliefs, negative thoughts, and emotions that holds us in the lower-vibration pattern.

Fortunately, we have a great deal of help in making the transition to a higher vibration. Beings from higher dimensional realms are present to assist us. We simply need to ask for their help and become aware of the flooding of divine light and love that is currently arriving from the cosmos. Releasing old patterns and negative emotions gets easier if we have a clear intention of letting them go.

Egyptian numerology is a fabulous tool that enables us to get a glimpse of what our life courses will take once aligned with the fifth dimension. It is the number frequencies that hold the potential and inherent abilities hidden in our birth charts and the arithmancy of our birth certificate names.

The information regarding numerology has changed over the past decade and now gives us access to higher frequencies not available to us before this time. It is imperative that we emerge with this new intelligence and ancient wisdom, for we are the ones we have been waiting for. It reminds us to reach for the stars and not settle for the dust—and when there is no leader to follow, we must become one.

PART IV

CHAPTER 19

Sacred Oracle Word

Arithmancy of Our Birth Names

The arithmancy of our birth names is the process in numerology of assigning a numeric calculation value to each letter of the alphabet. Our birth certificate names are as important as our birth dates. We decode the specific meanings within our names through the dynamic process of arithmancy.

Some people think that because our birth dates and birth names are chosen for us—as in planned cesarean births and the names that generally our parents settle on—there may not be anything sacred about these them, but the ancients believe that nothing is random.

The mother linked to the soul in her womb from the moment of conception has a delicate hand in the process of identifying the energy within her. It is believed the incoming soul communicates to the mother or both parents during pregnancy through a psychic link and that this determines pertinent birth information, including birth date, time, name, location, health, and more.

I recommend pregnant women keep a diary of daily alterations to her thoughts, feelings, decisions, books she feels guided to read, creative aspirations, cultural preferences, and spiritual guidance during her gestation. I passionately believe a mother can tell much about the unborn child through her intuitive perceptions.

When I was pregnant with my daughter, I was guided to travel to New Zealand. I read *Autobiography of a Yogi* by Paramahansa Yogananda for the first time, and all I craved was Indian food. I felt that all this information was transferred to me through my pregnancy and I was being navigated in preparation to receive important instructions that would help me understand the life that was growing inside of me.

In many societies, the naming of a child is conducted by the mother because she has the greatest attunement to the incarnating soul, and even though a priest or priestess of our society plays a major role, the mother ultimately has the final word.

The ancients recognized the season of pregnancy as a very mystical time. It is when the parents attune themselves to the incoming soul and become channels. They discern the energies and purpose of the name that assists in the manifestation of the child's highest potential.

When we were born, we were all assigned our oracle words. These magical words are our birth names. All words can be magical, according to how much spiritual significance we desire to attach to them. If used within the proper manner, they open up tremendous spiritual wisdom. Learning the physical and spiritual powers plus energy inherent within our names leads us to see our reflections of energies, gifts, potential, capabilities, and karma.

Our names give us power to balance our physical and spiritual bodies, awakening our highest abilities and potential. We use our names for energy, beauty, power, love, and prosperity. These words have unlimited possibilities and are available for those willing to put forth the effort to learn how to use them.

Tradition states that when we learn to align our energies and perceptions with divine energies inherent in and reflected through our names, it opens communication with angelic beings who have chosen to work with us through our creative expression in this incarnation, and these beings are known as our guardian angels.

Our names reflect the personal magic we project out into the world, and this significant source of power is effective through the arithmancy of our birth certificate names, determining the heart's desire, personality, and destiny frequencies, guiding us to clearer meaning in and direction of our lives. The names on our birth certificates represent the legal, rooted, physical grounding of our energies here in physical life. Our names hold sacred frequencies and vibrations that identify us by sound.

Some of the key concepts in numerology have to do with *frequency, vibration,* and *energy.* Pythagoras reminds us that sound, tone, and frequency carry vibration and are imprinted with meaning, integrity, and influence. When our names are spoken, they carry personal resonance frequencies.

Sound is a direct link between humanity and the Divine. All the ancient mystery schools taught their students the use of sound as a creative healing force, and it is the oldest form of healing, a predominant part in the early teachings of the Greeks, Chinese, East Indians, Tibetans, Egyptians, American Indians, Mayas, and Aztecs.

Our birth names are used in the arithmancy of our charting calculations, but primary, spiritual, nicknames, surnames, and married names additionally reveal much about people.

I believe our birth names are sacred and each name has a numeric resonance frequency aligned with the soul's contract. Our names reflect the energy signatures and patterns needed to unfold, expand, and overcome within this lifetime. Numerology, nameology, and arithmancy are based on the idea that each soul comes into this world to learn certain lessons, achieve specific goals, and experience overall development that propels evolution.

Learning to work with the power in our names released from our souls and into our lives is the purpose of this work. Researching the esoteric significance and use of our names as a tool for enlightenment and attainment was once a part of the ancient spiritual science taught within the Atlantean wisdom temples, and for the new age disciple, it must again form a part of our educational process.

When I chart using the frequencies of the birth name, it gives me crucial knowledge regarding the direction a soul chose to take in this lifetime. The ancients recognized that knowing the name of something is to have knowledge and power over it, but it implies knowing all aspects of that name. Our individual names contain much power, and coming to know them properly, we discover much about our own souls' growth, their purposes, and how to release our spiritual energies more effectively into the physical world. The meaning, sounds, rhythms, and nature of the letters and their combinations all disclose secrets about individuals' essences—past, present, and future, physical and spiritual. We are an integration of past energies and experiences, and the potential creativity within our personalities is reflected within the names we have chosen for this incarnation.

Unlike our birthdates, our first and middle names are chosen for us by someone else, most likely by our parents. Our last names are hereditary and handed down through the generations. Our first names are our social names, and our middle names are our soul names.

I believe every given birth name and frequency contains divine essence regardless of who delivers it to us. Some people are inspired to change their birth names and live with entirely different frequencies later in life. Although such a name change is significant numerically, it is the birth certificate name that determines one's destiny. The name change is calculated as an influential, supplemental, or additional frequency that is added to the original birth certificate name.

I had a client contact me once and say that she did not know her birth certificate name because she'd been adopted. All she had to go by was her adopted name. I told her that I believe everything happens for a reason and, therefore, we should use the only name she had available. If circumstances warrant that we are not given information for one reason or another, as in this case, I honor the process.

On the other hand, if our parents had in mind for us names different from those on our birth certificates, I would use those names instead. Those are the names more intricately linked between parents and children.

When people come to me to change their names because they believe the frequencies of their birth names are stopping them from achieving success, romance, and abundance, I explain that Egyptian numerology does not believe in the duality of numbers, meaning the concept of good and bad number frequencies. Instead, I offer to work with individuals to help them understand their birth names and how they can use their unique abilities, talents, and gifts to attract their hearts' desires.

Changing the frequency of your birth name will not magically attract you to money, success, or romance, and it does not delete and void the vibration of your birth name. There is a lot of information to consider before we change our names for material gain. It is much easier to unfold the power within our given names than to take on new ones. Changing names is not like changing clothes that are worn out or do not seem to fit us anymore; our names are intimate links to our highest essences.

Numbers are vibrational, like color, sound, animals, and various forms of energy. Once we understand their meaning and power, we utilize these for our benefit and personal magic. We use them to alter our state of consciousness once we understand the value of the frequencies we desire to attract.

Every number frequency has universal laws hidden within its structure. Changing our names without knowing all the ramifications would be like giving a toddler a torch gun to light a candle.

Egyptian numerology honors the integrity of our names and the energies they represent. If you want to attract a relationship, make sure you have self-love. If you want to attract prosperity, make sure you are balanced in the saving and spending aspects of abundance. If you want to attract success, make sure you are in integrity with the laws of energy.

Meaning of the Vowels in Our Names

The voice is a powerful instrument for healing. Pythagoras recognized the therapeutic potential of speech and treated diseases through the reading of poetry. He taught his students how a well- modulated voice with pleasing words and soft meter restored balance to the body, heart, mind, and soul.

When using mantras, we tap into the mystical power hidden inside the syllables of specific words, and reciting these words repeatedly creates a momentum of intentions powered by the force within the recited words.

Our speech is composed of two elements: (1) vowels and (2) consonants. The vowel sounds are the most important aspect of the spoken sound because without them the consonants would not be sounded. Many of the early alphabets excluded the vowels because it was believed that they were too provocative, causing specific inner forces to be energized. Every letter or combination of letters has great significance. The Chaldean alphabet, one of the forerunners of our alphabet, was devised as a tool for attaining higher wisdom. The letters, sounds, glyphic forms, and their numerological equivalences provide portals to the archetypal energies operating and motivated through words.

In Egyptian numerology, the heart's desire is the numeric calculation of the vowels of the birth certificate name. The vowels in our names are fluid and soft, describing the deepest passions and motivators of our hearts. They hold our true vision of what we came here to do in this lifetime.

It is where we hold what is sacred to our hearts, and it is the frequency of our heart body and what motivates our passions, purposes, and beliefs. It signifies our authenticity and triggers us to stay in alignment with our soul contracts.

It is inspired and ignited by an awakening, and until then, it directs our experiences toward maturation, teaching us who we are and why we are here.

Because this vibration is linked to our hearts, we access it only when our hearts are open. Anything blocking us from the flow of feelings causes us to formulate our experiences through our minds, leading to imbalance, because it does not allow the heart energy bodies to mature, and this is why an awakening can be painful.

The walls around our hearts need to come down, whether by a feather or sledgehammer. Keeping our hearts initiated is the journey after our eyes are opened.

Meaning of the Consonants in Our Names

The personality or expression number is the arithmancy of the consonants in one's birth certificate name. Our expressions define how we bring the heart's desire into manifestation in the material world. The vowels maintain the fluidity of our names, and the consonants are the forms by which the vowels are expressed.

The personalities are like the clothes we wear; they protect us, define us, or both. Personas are complements to the inner aspects of our selves. They portray our personal style and behaviors and how we imagine and present ourselves to the world on both the conscious and the unconscious levels.

Our expressions describe learned behaviors and how we use them to express our essential selves. Our personas are built from experience, which is feedback the universe gives us about our choices, feelings, thoughts, words, and actions. This is especially important in the analysis of how present we are in the process of creating our destinies.

Our heart's desire numbers are the essences of our true selves, and our personality numbers are the frequencies at which we choose the world to view us. These are our full expressions of being humans in the physical form. They are how we protect, express, and manifest our hearts' desires.

Once we understand the essences of these frequencies, we appreciate the magic and source of power used to influence the outside world and evaluate the gifts and talents used when expressing our creativity.

The personality or expression number is the initial vibration that people, animals, environments, plants, and spirits pick up from us organically. It is the base energy they use to psychically tell whether we are authentic about who we are, what we are doing, and our true intentions. If we are not in alignment with these frequencies, they will sense it, and something will just feel *off*.

These are our energetic personality blueprints, and when we are in integrity with the vibrations we emit, our auras strengthen, expand, and become brighter. People, animals, and the environment around us will feel invited, interested, and attracted. They will trust, feel safe around, and open up to us naturally.

First, Middle, and Last Names

The three major names we carry in our lifetimes are the first names (social), middle names (soul), and last names (hereditary).

Our first names are our social names and indicate the personal and individual lessons we are here to learn and act on. These are the sounds that project our signature vibrations and how we are viewed and received in a cordial manner. These are the energies we reflect out to the world in greeting and to form relationships. They reflect our strengths, creativity, and personal power. Our first names are how our parents chose to respond to us, and they trigger our social acceptance and even expectations. Many people change or modify their first names, which reflect specific aspects of our lives.

Our middle names are our soul names, and they are linked to inner guidance. They are windows to our souls and hold the secret to our healing, enlightenment, and pure essences.

These frequencies are spiritual names and in essence hold the truth we carry about our souls' incarnations. These are the aspects about us that nobody sees but the very nature behind our breath, beliefs, actions, and what we consider precious and closest to our hearts. These are the placeholders for our true and authentic selves regardless of what other people think about us. They are reminders to keep our soul-life purposes in alignment with Source regardless of the circumstances our social roles play. If we think about it, these are the names not too many people know about us, except for our parents, our family members, and people with whom we are involved in close relationships. They are silent socially, but the vibrations speak volumes about everything we believe, think, say, and do. Some people choose their middle names as their primary names, disregarding their first names entirely. When this happens, it does not alter the arithmancy of their birth certificate names but changes the position of the nameology meaning, where the middle names become their social vibrations.

Our last names, family names, or surnames are called the hereditary, genetic, or karmic frequencies given to us at birth and indicate the energies inherited from our ancestors, karma associated with our family, and the qualities most available to us through family heritage. All these contribute and shape the expressions of our individual creative essences.

We are born into karmic frequencies from both parents. The vibration lineage appears to be dominating on the paternal side because the woman typically takes her husband's surname, although this has been changing with time. Our last names are not chosen for us but rather handed down from one generation to another. When a woman marries and takes her husband's last name, her original birth-name frequency stays with her for life, and she inevitably adopts the hereditary energy of her husband's lineage as a supplemental or additional vibration.

In Egyptian numerology, it is suggested for a woman to keep her maiden name or hyphenate the two last names and not completely drop her birth last name, because it represents and holds the memories of her destiny.

If a woman takes on only her husband's name, there is a chance that her destiny will be redirected toward her husband's family karma and not her own. But we all have free will and can choose for ourselves what feels right.

Use the following arithmancy guide to break down the numeric calculation of letters to numbers, add each number and break down the total to a single-digit number unless it is a master number.

I have further instructions and information in my book *Egyptian Numerology: Emergence into the Fifth Dimension*.

1	2	3	4	5	6	7	8	9
A	B	C	D	E	F	G	H	I
J	K	L	M	N	O	P	Q	R
S	T	U	V	W	X	Y	Z	

The name Kirsten Ryan Bachmeier would be calculated as:

2	9	9	1	2	5	5		9	7	1	5		2	1	3	8	4	5	9	5	9
K	I	R	S	T	E	N		R	Y	A	N		B	A	C	H	M	E	I	E	R

First name: Kirsten = 2 + 9 + 9 + 1 + 2 + 5 + 5 = **33/6**

Middle name: Ryan = 9 + 7 + 1 + 5 = **22/4**

Last name: Bachmeier = 2 + 1 + 3 + 8 + 4 + 5 + 9 + 5 + 9 = 46 (4 + 6 = 10)/10 = **1**

Total: 6 + 4 + 1 = **11/2**

Arithmancy Numerical Characteristics

Name 1: Independent, Assertive, Intelligent, Creative, and Intuitive

You have a strong and determined nature that keeps you focused on your goals. These are leadership qualities. You appear to be independent and self-sustaining, or at least you strive to be. You are a creative thinker and enjoy the analytical approach to solving challenges.

Because of your high intelligence, you enjoy strategic opportunities to advance your curiosity. Your assertive behavior is appreciated in the business world, and your loyalty is admired among friends.

You are intuitive and have psychic abilities that are faithful guides throughout your life journey. These are qualities guiding you to rare opportunities, and you are encouraged to develop these gifts to the highest degree possible. They are assets to your continued success in life.

Name 2: Creative, Romantic, Diplomatic, Loving, and Empathic

It is evident that relationships are an extremely important aspect of your life. You are friendly and easy to be around, and everyone enjoys your company. Your diplomatic nature finds you invited to social gatherings, especially those that need an artful approach to problem solving. You have a creative flair and are an accomplished artist in one or many fields.

Romance, beauty, art, and music are all activities that stimulate your senses, adding to your charming personality. You thrive in surroundings where there are peace, love, and harmony, desiring to reflect these elements into your environment wherever you go.

You are empathic and take an emotional and intuitive approach to life in general. You think with your heart most of the time, and this proves to be a faithful guide. It is your ability to feel so deeply that gives you the lead when it comes to understanding others and developing connections that can be trusted, accepted, and followed. You have a loving personality, making you approachable and helpful to many people.

Name 3: Social, Expressive, Intuitive, Creative, and Joyful

Self-expression is only one of your many talents. Whether you choose to express yourself in art form, social activities, or literary composition, you have a unique ability to squeeze out your creative juices for others to taste and savor. You intuitively bring joy to others, making their lives more meaningful and productive. You are a social butterfly who brings laughter and brightness to every person and function that you come in contact with.

You are highly creative and have a gift of communicating with children and animals. You are able to relate to their innocence and appreciate their closeness to Spirit. These are qualities you possess within your own personality, and it reflects through your pureness of heart. Joy is an emotion you embody, and giving freely with those you love and care for makes your heart sing.

Sometimes this frequency can hide insecurities that no one else can see. It is important your light and joyful expression takes time out to heal old wounds to strengthen your inner core.

Name 4: Honesty, Loyalty, Meticulous, Developer, and Perseverance

Although found to thrive under routine and order, you have a creative mind that loves to color outside the lines. You have an active imagination to envision possibilities that have not yet surfaced for the average population to see. Once you have set your heart, mind, and spirit on achieving a goal, your perseverance acts in overdrive to accomplish the task.

This frequency is usually known for its developing and building traits, and often overlooked are your intuition and psychic abilities. When focused on healing, you have a natural talent for demonstrating meticulous attention to energy. You can effortlessly tap into the four elements (i.e., fire, air, water, and earth) and apply healing where it is needed. Your honesty and loyalty serve as a grounding force for those you love and care for.

This frequency is solid, strong, and secure, knowing that a strong foundation is crucial in every area of life. Family plays an important role, and oftentimes, it is the root or source you go back to for reassurance, answers, and comfort in your daily challenges.

Name 5: Friendly, Busy, Inquisitive, Adventurer, and Service Oriented

You have a warm, friendly, and social disposition that thrives in emergencies where you can practice your art of intuitive problem-solving skills and demonstrate the love for selfless service.

Your free-spirited nature finds you traveling for pleasure or business without a second thought to a secure home life. You are adaptable in all motions of change, and for you, sitting still is unproductive and a little boring. Although you have a strong independent streak, you desire partnership with a significant other. The problem is finding someone who understands your adventurous lifestyle and will not tie you down to a monotonous future.

You are curious by nature and thrive on learning. We can most likely find you reading three to five books at a time, alternating them without a desire to get to the ending. You are known for your creativity and your healing qualities. Because of your intuition and intense closeness to Spirit, you can apply your gifts in the art of helping others. You are a channel for Higher Source to work through, and your generous heart always accepts the challenge.

Personal power is important, and you thrive when applying your intellect with your creative modalities. You are strong and innovative, with a powerful drive toward healing and leadership. Your life journey includes using your abilities to help yourself and others.

Name 6: Nurturing, Intuitive, Domestic, Healer, and Adviser

There is a soft and gentle nature about you. People trust and gather around you like fairies surround the wise old oak tree. This is pleasing and feeds your nurturing qualities, allowing you to practice skills of intuitive divine wisdom.

You are domestic and family oriented, with a strong sense of responsibility. Although your creativity can be witnessed in your home decor, clothing style, and artistic abilities, your real talent lies in the ability to help others. The love and light you emanate opens your heart to channel, and you intuitively know how to funnel Source's healing grace through your hands and heart while extending them out to others. Your observant and empathic abilities allow you to guide people in times of need. Whether you council, pray, or give hands-on healing, your gifted insight goes toward benefiting those who suffer.

You enjoy caretaking and finding ways to make life bearable to the less fortunate. The most important lesson in this lifetime is the nurturing of your own soul. It will be important for you to set healthy boundaries and put yourself among the ones who need spiritual nourishment. Once you do this, you will lead most by example. This is the way of the ascended masters.

Name 7: Genius, Spiritual, Reclusive, Naturalist, and Psychic

You do not keep stock in earthly matters but rather have a rare connection to planetary involvement. One might say that you came from another planet or you perceive wisdom from a higher source. Both of these explanations might be correct.

You get your power mostly from nature, and you enjoy quiet moments of solitude where you can easily access and commune with Spirit. You are quite intelligent and crave the necessary mental stimuli to keep you entertained. You have a reserved quality about you that others may interpret as reclusive, but the solitary life is complimentary, comfortable, and productive for you.

You have a spiritual link to the other realms that entices your intuition and psychic abilities. Understanding the concealed and mysterious is in your second nature, and being true to yourself is number one. This frequency is common among priests, priestesses, druids, and spiritual advisers. It is the energy of the **mystical and magical, seeking purpose** in being illuminated with higher wisdom and divine truth.

You are most comfortable in the land called the *dream time* or *in-between time*, where beings from other worlds can introduce themselves and visit with you when called on. Your curiosity about unveiled dimensions becomes a reality when you allow yourself to be open and vulnerable to all possibilities.

Name 8: Business, Energetic, Communication, Abundance, and Caution

You have a gift for attracting opportunities that enhance your energy flow. You are energetically inspired when focusing on one or more creative projects. When your wheels start turning, you tend to need less sleep than the average person and can become completely immersed in the energy flow needed to produce the desired outcome of your attention. This makes you a particularly good partner in business arrangements and financial endeavors that require the utmost dedication to detailed-orientated maneuvers.

You have excellent communication skills and know how to express yourself to draw people closer to your enormous energy field. You are highly resourceful, and when you learn how to balance energy flow, you understand the importance of giving back more than you receive as described in the laws of attraction. If you block your energy, it can become detrimental to your health and overall well-being.

Being cautious is part of your nature, and it is important to protect your valuable assets even when they relate to your personal life. Even though it is wise to protect your delicate balance of abundance when allowing others into your affairs, make certain it does not turn into paranoia. If you develop your integrity, honesty, and open heart, the universe always provides accordingly.

Name 9: Compassionate, Reserved, Spiritual, Creative, and Humanitarian

Even when you were young, you were observed by others as a wise old soul. You have sage-like qualities that leave a certain sparkle in your eyes. Some people acquire higher wisdom with age and experience, but you were born with it.

You have a natural compassion for people, animals, and our environment. It is important to use your passionate dreams for bringing healing and clarity to unfortunate beings. You have leadership and humanitarian skills that are quite evident in your immediate surroundings, and if they are not evident yet, you will find ways to install them.

It is instinctive for you to be reserved and somewhat of a loner. You did not inherit the insecurities that would make you dependent on anyone. You have high ideals with a great imagination and are extremely intuitive. With these gifts intact, you must reserve alone time to process and balance your delicate nature.

You are naturally attracted to a spiritual way of life. Everything your heart stands for is divinely induced and guided. Leadership, healing, and artistic talents are part of your life mission. You have many creative gifts and expressing your love and appreciation through art form is a natural outlet for your compassionate nature.

Name 11: Intuitive, Creative, Healer, Psychic, and Aware

Your energy is a higher frequency of the number 2 and twice as strong as the number 1. Having two 1s side by side is a symbol of a double antennae and a channel to spiritual awareness. This manifests itself in many ways, but whatever form it takes, it suggests an abundance of creativity. You will be strong and independent with substantial intuition. You possess psychic abilities that probably will not develop completely until you are older. As you mature, you will inherit a flair for the arts, writing, and guiding people to evolve spiritually and emotionally. These are the natural gifts you will develop, practice, and establish as they become important skills adding to your accomplishments.

Because you serve as a double conduit to higher awareness, you are a healing channel for spirit. You will do this through psychic counseling, remote viewing, or hands-on restoration. Even your creative endeavors have healing power when developing your imagination and unlocking your magical capabilities. When you believe and act on your dreams, inspirations, and visions, they will lead you into other worlds where Spirit is waiting to guide you.

You can become reserved, as you are an original thinker and do not put a lot of investment in the material world. You enjoy sharing ideas and inspirations with like-minded individuals, but you save alone time for yourself, and this is something you innately identify with. You are at home around anything that is nonjudgmental and finds expression through the powers of the soul. You find comfort in nature, beauty, and the animal kingdom. All these speak a native language derived from the heart, which will be processed through and into your creative nature.

Name 22: Manifestation, Beauty, Connection, and Intuition

You have the power to connect many forces and design your intentions in your mind and materialize them in outside world. As a cultivator, you learn early in life how to manifest and materialize your heart's desire. Another equally important quality that you possess is the ability to see, feel, and hear beauty on a deep and profound level. It is important to build with a sense of harmony, peace, understanding, and compassion, and in this way, you will be utilizing the dust stars are made of.

You are phenomenally successful but cannot achieve your grand designs by working alone. You can be very practical in nature and possess extreme potential when working alongside others. You bring qualities of insight, talent, courage, intelligence, power, and charisma to your elaborate plans and are encouraged to complete tasks with noble intentions and for the betterment of everyone involved.

You battle lifelong challenges around balancing mental, physical, and emotional standpoints. You might be overwhelmed with your gifts and develop a negative outlook. This is detrimental because your thoughts have immeasurable power and are used to create your reality. If you learn to hone your abilities, then any ambitious vision, no matter how large, can be attained. Your potential is virtually limitless. It is important you maintain a powerfully optimistic outlook and avoid the need for power and greed at all costs. When your dark side is embraced, you are focused on the advancement of others.

You are influenced by the number 4 and behold the qualities of reliability, discipline, logic, and conscientiousness. These immense traits help inspire your vibration. Number 22 is considered to be the most powerful value in numerology, so you will experience vast success and support during your lifetime. The 22, known as the *master cultivator*, has retained some of the desirable characteristics from the master number 11 and the number 4, aiding in amplifying its potency.

When you are balanced, you have immense psychic and intuitive powers. You carry the qualities of an old soul when living up to your full potential and create a bridge between the divine and humanity. Your purpose is to assist others in spiritual transformation by maintaining this bridge which allows healing, peace, and higher energies to emerge here on earth.

Name 33: Visionary, Creative, Expression, and Healer

Besides being a channel for Spirit, you express yourself best by teaching others. Your superpowers are communication, expression, sensitivity, and creativity.

You have a childlike wonder and curiosity filled with joy, love, and beauty. Your intuition and empathy keep you connected to your friends, family, and community. We may find you in a healing, advising, or creative field, where caring and nurturing others predominates your other skills.

I call the number 6 the "Lighthouse" because you are a beacon of light here on earth, attracting others toward the truth and ingenuity of your own divine nature. Master number 33 adds up to the number 6 and in its purest form is a higher manifestation of the number 6.

Thirty-three is the number of the master teacher. This number brings to light the statement "We are the ones we've been waiting for." Yours is the path of divine expression and power of the spoken word. The master number 33 guides, heals, directs, and restores people with its altruistic powers and rather high energy. You have the gifts of imagination, dream materialization, and illumination, which are the accumulations of all three master numbers combined. Einstein said, "Imagination is everything. It is the preview of life's coming attractions." Your journey includes raising awareness and consciousness, uplifting, and bringing joyful loving energy to the world. By embracing and balancing your 33 energy here on earth, you are bringing the world into a natural state of order.

Your mission is to be a masterful healer and an inspired visionary. This is a spiritual avenue that encourages you to tap into your creativity. emotional maturity, nurturing nature, and healing presence. The implication of the master numbers is developed and refined over time like a fine wine. The 33/6 is specifically set up where you must first and foremost *heal yourself*. You will be put into situations that require you to deal with responsibility—taking responsibility for yourself and your actions, not taking on the responsibilities of others and becoming a martyr, enabler, or controller.

It is your quest to teach and lead by example through the power of love. You are meant to serve as a conduit for healing by whatever modality you feel most compelled to engage in. This master number is preconditioned for leadership positions and encompasses visionary goals, truth, beauty, and a nurturing open heart. There are countless ways to act on your master energies and being in alignment with your 33 means you are focused on giving, and if you are not focused on giving, you are not in alignment with your ultimate goals.

The bottom line is that you are serving your highest when embracing and acting on your sense of masterful healing and inspired vision. You are a natural nurturer and have a gift for healing on both personal and grand scales. This is no easy task, because it requires having both feet on the ground, viewing the world in a realistic way, and not getting fed up or disappointed when the world does not meet your level of high expectations.

You are at your best when serving others and able to act on your heart-centered vision for the world.

<u>CHAPTER 20</u>

Inner Guidance

Akashic Record

A spirit council meets with our souls when we are ready to incarnate into the next lifetime. They review our past lives with us, as well as any karmic debts we have accrued, and help determine the best procedure and process to take in order to balance out our karma, and if we are assigned to specific life duties that will enhance and benefit the world, they help lay out the courses our lives will take. In this arrangement, we determine who our parents and family members will be and where we will be born. Those of the spirit council assist us by mapping out our numerical and astrological frequencies, which determine our souls' urges, life paths, karmic lessons, and life purposes through our birthdays, months, and years. They form our hearts' desires, personalities, and destinies through our birth certificate names. All our karmic-debt circumstances are laid out in events and timelines, we set up trigger points (cycles) that lead us in the right direction, and we are assigned guardian angels and guides to help us succeed once we have landed back here on earth. Everything is recorded in our personal akashic library.

Many ancient cultures have reported the existence of the akashic records. *Akasha* is a Sanskrit word meaning "sky," "space," or "ether." The akashic records are said to be a collection of wisdom stored in the ether, akashic field, or zero-point field and have existed since the beginning of time. Quantum scientists are now recognizing that the akasha, as recorded by the ancients, is an energy field that connects all living things.

In theosophy and anthroposophy, the akashic records are a compendium of all our human events, thoughts, words, emotions, and intents ever to have occurred in the past, present, and future. The hall, or library, of the akashic records is where all souls' records are stored energetically. Everything that has happened, is happening, and can happen is recorded in this book, and this field is continuously written and rewritten every day. The existence of such energetic records has been known by people worldwide and is called by various other names, including the "book of life" in the Bible.

We have our own masters, teachers, and beings of light keeping track of our records. We can access these masters and teachers, and they will answer our personal questions about this life and past lives that are affecting us today. When we realize that we came into this life with plans, to complete karma, fulfill past-life vows, be with special people, and support people who are part of our soul families, the meanings of our lives become transparent and clear. The human challenge is that as soon as we are born, we forget our plans, and at times in our lives, we may feel blocked, constricted, or disappointed because we don't remember why we chose our families, our situations, or the circumstances we find ourselves in. Accessing these akashic records or encoding our frequencies through Egyptian numerology helps us learn information about these situations, advances our healing, and clears emotional pain. It leads to answers relating to health, career, relationships, life purpose, self-esteem, abundance, and much more.

Inner-Guidance Numbers

One's inner guidance is essentially one's higher self. These number frequencies are what our higher selves use to solve our life challenges or bring answers to difficult internal questions. These are the vibrations we respond to when we need inner guidance. They are derived from our doubling our destiny numbers. We use the frequencies off our spiritual or confirmation names by calculating the arithmancy. There are guides that come to us through other means, and if they reveal their names to us, we can calculate those frequencies in the same way.

Spirit guides are incorporeal beings assigned to us before birth. We all have individual spirit helpers looking after us, and they are always here to guide, protect, and support us. Our spirit guides bring wisdom and perspective of many lifetimes, and their purpose is to guide us through life to achieve our highest purposes on our souls' journeys. These guides are responsible for helping us fulfill the soul contracts, sacred treaties, or soul-life agreements we made before incarnation.

Our guardian angels stay with us throughout our entire lives, and some guides accompany us throughout our life journeys while others only enter every now and again to assist in clarifying specific areas of our lives or goals that we are in the process of achieving. They can vary at levels of consciousness. Some may be ascended masters (such as Jesus), and others might be deceased relatives. They may be spirits who have had physical incarnations, enlightened beings from other planets, or angels who have never incarnated before.

The average person has approximately six spirit guides. I did not learn about mine all at once. It took time and many psychic readings to become aware of my invisible helpers. I have two spirit guides, named Ivan and Eric, who are in charge of the timing and planning of events that occur in my life. Their job is to make sure everything shows up on my timeline, so I don't miss important opportunities. There is King Charles IV, who governs my love life because he has a karmic debt to repay from many lifetimes ago, and he along with other guides are involved in bringing opportunities of possible love and joy into my life. I have Archangel Raphael, who assists in teaching me how to be a healer; Gabriel, who is teaching me about giving and receiving messages; and Metatron, who is helping me with my writing and life purpose. Situational guides are Ascended Masters Kuthumi, El Morya, and Lady Isis, who have chimed in to help me write about Egyptian numerology, along with Edgar Cayce, Paramahansa Yogananda, my deceased father, and many more. In my first book, I write more about some of these beings and spirits, and as always, my deep gratitude for their guidance and presence fills my heart.

Inner-Guidance Number

Numerology of Spiritual Names

In different cultures, there is a particular age and ceremony marking an individual's path into a spiritual journey. Even if we do not belong to a culture assigning us the privilege of spiritual ceremony, we may be given names (other than our birth names) that allow us to celebrate marks in time toward spiritual evolution. In Catholicism, a confirmation name is given to an adolescent; in the Jewish culture, it is a bar or bat mitzvah; and in Native American tribes, they call it a rite of passage.

The average age for culture recognition into adulthood and spirituality is twelve. We can be given confirmation or spiritual names at any age, and these names can be given to us by a tribe, or we select the names by individual preference. The number 12 signifies a portal in time. It is a time of change that ignites one's destiny, and in some cultures, this is the age where a child begins adulthood. Not only does puberty play an important role in children's lives by changing their bodies, but it triggers the outside world to begin accumulating events that form and change individuals' complete lifetimes, setting the tone toward their personal destinies. (Refer to chapter 22, "Transformative Years."

I've conducted a personal study proving, in frequent cases, a significant event occurs in the lives of people between the ages of twelve and fourteen that marks an essential change in their lives, imprinting the beginning of emotional maturity. This change comes in the structure of a divorce, marriage, birth, relocation, school transfer, death, or severe illness and takes place with at least one major family member. Regardless of this specific event, the impact is great enough to alter individuals' lives and set the emotional stage for their future years. Eventually, this encounter is strong enough to carve the layers necessary to forge the path toward one's destiny. The number 12 not only is a destiny trigger but also represents a cycle year, months in a year calendar, hours on the face of a clock, the number of Jesus's disciples, and the number of members on a court jury. Most important, it is the Egyptian numerology number of a master.

In the Catholic religion, a person can choose a spiritual name through the sacrament of confirmation. This is a time in individuals' lives when the church recognizes the rite of passage into adulthood and asks initiates to confirm their faith by choosing saints to be their life guardians. I use this example because it was my childhood path, and I am familiar with it. Although this name is supplementary to your birth certificate name, it is valued as your inner-guidance name and has a numerical value that is important to recognize. It is also the frequency of your own personal magic.

We calculate our inner-guidance numbers by doubling our destiny numbers off the arithmancy from our birth certificate names. Both forms of calculation are correct. For instance, the patron saint name I choose when I was confirmed in the Catholic religion at age twelve was Saint Anne. When I use the arithmancy chart, I calculate this name to add up to the number 7. The name Saint has the value of the number 9 and will stand up next to any other number in integrity. My destiny number is the master number 11/2. When I double this number, it brings my inner-guidance number to the master number 22/4. I interpret this as Saint Anne using the power of the master number 22/4 to work with the number 7.

If you do not have a spiritual name, use the calculation of doubling your destiny number and reducing it to a single-digit unless it's a master number, 11/2, 22/4, 33/6, or some such. This will be the frequency that your inner guidance uses when it works with you. If you do not know the name of your inner guidance, use the following meditation to learn who it is, and then calculate the vibration.

Inner-Guidance Name Meditation

Creating the Inner Sanctuary to Meet Spirit Guides

An effective way to increase awareness of our spirit guides is by creating special sanctuaries within our minds and consciousness where we can go to initiate communion with them. We use our imaginations in creating the sanctuaries and design places where we can visualize and feel comfortable and protected. They can be temple scenes, places out in nature, or castles in the clouds. They are places of intersection where the physical and spiritual realms meet. We develop points in our hearts and minds where there is a thinning of veils between the two worlds.

These are places where those in Spirit approach us on our own terms. The more we develop them in our minds, the stronger our Spirit contact will be. The sanctuaries are sacred spaces, and we can create and change them as we go along. Initially, we may wish to use the following scenario but not lock ourselves into it. It is to serve as a guideline to help us begin to build our own inner spirit sanctuaries.

1. Begin the exercise by making sure you will not be interrupted or disturbed. Turn your phone off.
2. Set the atmosphere with candles, incense, or other fragrances.
3. Close your eyes and relax by performing a progressive relaxation technique or some form of rhythmic breathing. The more relaxed you are, the easier it is to access the subconscious mind and stimulate spirit contact.

4. Now visualize the following scenario. Use your imagination and make it real with the creative power of your mind.

As you relax, draw all your energies around you, as if someone placed a comfortable old quilt around your shoulders. You are relaxed and at peace. There is a sense of anticipation, for you are about to be introduced to one of your spirit guides. Within the darkness of mind, a scene begins to form. Faintly, you hear the sound of water, a soft, gentle stream that is close by. Hear the sound of birds as you begin to feel the warmth of the sun on your skin. Smell the gentle scent of spring flowers and newly mown hay as a soft breeze caresses your face. Look around and see that you are in a small circular garden and the color of flowers stand out against the greens of grasses and trees.

Surrounding the garden are oak trees, and their branches extend out as if protecting you. Breathe deeply of the sweet air. You are relaxed and at peace. You know this place. You have been here before. Maybe in your dreams or maybe in a distant lifetime. You just know that it is your special haven. It is a place where you can go to heal and refresh yourself, and it is a place of sacred life and peace. You see that you are sitting on a stone. It seems to have been carved out into a chair for you within this garden. Touching the stone makes you feel solid and connected to the earth. As you look about, renewing your memories of the sanctuary, you see a path that leads down from a distant mountain to this garden. This path is lined with stones of every color and kind. At the opposite side of the garden, this path continues and leads out from the garden down to a distant valley. As you look down this path, you see your present home within that distant valley and understand that you are at a plateau, an intersection of time and space.

It is an inner sanctuary where the real and unreal meet. It is an interception of the finite and infinite, the physical and spiritual, and knowing this is an exhilarating feeling. It relieves you of stress and worry. In this place, you only have to be. As you sit on your stone chair, you see up the path facing the mountain a small bright golden light. It draws closer and closer and floats gently up the path toward your little sanctuary. Its light is soft and gentle, yet it shines with a brilliance that you have never seen before. As it reaches the outer edge of your sanctuary, it stops, a large pulsating crystalline light. You watch, waiting, but it does not move. It stays just outside your garden, and this puzzles you at first, but then you remember that this is your garden, and nothing can enter without your permission. You find this thought to be very reassuring.

You slowly stand and take a step forward, and you nod your head with consent, acknowledging the light and giving it permission to enter. The light draws forward and hovers before you. The light shimmers with soft strands of gold streaming forth from it. The light seems to unfold itself like a flower blossoming, and as each petal of this light unfolds, you see that something or someone is inside. Then you see a wondrous being before you! See it. Imagine it and know that it is real.

As you look on this being, pay attention to what you experience. Are there specific colors? Fragrances? Do you feel a touch or tingling on any part of your body? Is it male or female? Even if the unfolding reveals only a symbol, that symbol can reflect a male or female energy. Trust your impressions, and begin to carry on a conversation with this being in your mind. Ask its name. What is its purpose? Why is it around you? How can you come to recognize it more consciously in the future? Do not force the answers. Let them come naturally. Let this being communicate itself to you and tell you why it is working with you and what it will help you accomplish in the future. Ask your guide how best to call on it in the future. Do not worry that you might be imagining it all, that it may all be a product of your imagination and not a reality. You would not be able to envision it at all if there was not something real about it. Now bring the conversation to a close and ask your guide for something that you can use to verify its reality. Is there something coming up in your life that you need to be aware of? Is there something important that you need to know? Ask it for a physical touch, a tingle, or some kind of physical sensation at a specific time over the next couple of days. Make it a reasonable request, one that is easily fulfilled and confirmed.

Now thank your guide for the opportunity to meet and work with it. As the golden light falls back up around your guide, send it off with your best thoughts and love.

As it withdraws from your garden, moving back down the path, sit back down on your rock. You now understand that in this inner sanctuary you can invite all your guides into your awareness. This is appealing, and you are excited about the opportunity of expanding your horizons.

You breathe deeply, relaxing and reliving the conversation in your mind. As you do, the garden begins to fade. You find yourself sitting in your home, comfortable and peaceful, remembering all that you have experienced. Slowly and gently open your eyes, aware for perhaps the first time that there is life and energy on all dimensions around you.

At this point, it is good to record your experience with your guides. Write down all that you saw, sensed, felt, or learned. This will help you in grounding your energies into the physical, and it helps remembering and identifying your individual guides. Also record any new impressions or symbols you may have received from this spirit guide. Sometimes insight into our spirit guides' energies comes when we are in the recording process. We understand more fully the information passed on to us during the encounter.

Fully center and ground yourself back into the physical. This can be accomplished by eating something or participating in some kind of physical activity.

Inner-Guidance Numbers

1

Your inner guidance is a leader, teacher, or researcher in a specific field of study. Although this frequency actively relates to research, mathematics, or music, it brings strength and ability to focus on any endeavor you are involved with. Your guidance will be clear, concise, and direct. The main purpose is to strengthen your connection to your spiritual journey and direct you toward areas in your life that will assist in completing your soul's destiny. You may be directed to build a healthy self-esteem in order to be a leader among your community. It will guide you into independence, show you how to express your creative nature, and help you become a force of nature once you tap into the gifts bestowed on your higher self. The energy is masculine.

2

This energy is showing up to bring balance into all areas of your life. It serves to enhance your creative abilities, such as design, art, composing, and writing. It magnifies intuition and increases psychic abilities. If there are concerns with codependency, addiction, or diabetes, this guidance is here to assist in overcoming such obstacles. The strengths of this frequency are in mediation and relationships. It shows up as a banner of peace, justice, and liberty and acts as a cocreator in business and personal affairs. Its purpose is to clarify duality and assist in abolishing judgment and shifting perspectives to a higher consciousness. The energy is feminine.

3

This is a frequency for bringing joy and the art of communication; healing the inner child; and encouraging creative performance. This guide ensures that joy comes to you from many sources. It shows up to comfort you if you have been depressed and serves as the inspiration for you to heal past wounds. If you have entertaining or performing gifts, it enhances your courage to go forward to succeed. Your guide showers you with social grace and gives you the gift of uplifting the people you care for. Your intuition will be heightened, which includes a strong relationship with children and animals. Creativity in self-expression is a must with this number. It is important that you continue your connection with elevating self-awareness and spiritual pursuits. It is both feminine and masculine.

4

This is a grounding force. It will assist in bringing stability, routine, and order to your life. It is an action and motivation number, supporting positive momentum within every project. It guides you to find the layers or procedure needed in the production of any project you are involved in. It provides a kinship with nature in all her healing properties and aids in forming relationships with the elementals, fairies, and leprechauns. This is the frequency of the druid and the priestess, and if you are a healer, this guidance benefits your study of anatomy and energy balancing. It is a vibration of loyalty and perseverance and is a hardworking number that doesn't mind getting its hands dirty. It is a masculine energy.

5

This guidance is here to help you adapt to any changes you are going through in life. It brings the currency of transformation wherever it goes, and it cleanses, purifies with a fire-flame frequency, and has the power to move through blocked energy. It is a force to be reckoned with and carries the inspiration of creation. It appears to clear the way of any obstruction in, through, and around your life, igniting the fires of creativity deep within your soul. If you need fire energy for your healing or to help heal someone else, this is the guidance for you. It guides you toward travel, culture, and education, and it advises, motivates, and leads you safely from one place to another. You are never meant to stay in one place when this guidance shows up. It is a feminine energy.

6

This is the vibration of universal love and harmony that appears to those who are natural healers, bringing gifts of intuition, empathy, and creativity. This is the number of the angels and ascended masters, guiding you to give messages to people who need to hear the truth, encouragement, and inspiration. It is a nurturing energy whose purpose is to open your heart, mind, and spirit to the celestial music and share it with the ones you love. When open to this guidance, you are directed into counseling, caretaking, and healing animals and people that are less fortunate than yourself. Practicing self-care is an important message given from this frequency, along with the lesson that we cannot give what we do not have. It is a feminine frequency.

7

This is a spiritual number, and its frequency is linked to our planetary system, especially the Pleiadians, Arcturians, and Syrians. A guide carrying this frequency shows you how to cross through the realms of time, space, and the dream time. You have a soul connection with this guide and a spiritual contract that specifically brought you together in this life to achieve a higher purpose. The joint mission is to show you various ways on how to connect to your spiritual support system in both; planetary hierarchy, angelic realm, elementals, and how to communicate with the spirit counsel. You have a sacred journey here on earth, and this guide assists in keeping you focused on your soul-life quest. It is a masculine number.

8

This guide leads you to a life of prosperity, resources, and abundance. The area of your life that benefits most when dealing with abundance will be the focal point of energy exchange—and not necessarily finances. This guide brings opportunities to gather your resources and learn to give and receive in balance. You are learning about integrity, especially in the area of communication, attracting whatever you are focused on, and it is important to always speak your truth. When guidance is in action, pay particular attention to your source of income and how the magic of Spirit works through you and not from you. How can you use your resources to help build a better world? It is a masculine number.

9

This is a high frequency and a spiritual number, much like the number 7. Guidance is here to assist in the completion of a project and lead you in the process toward the evolution of your spiritual journey. This frequency carries the energy of integrity and justice and belongs to a high-office council member. The lesson this guidance uncovers for you is in forgiveness and compassion, leading you to a life of selfless service. It enhances your interest in meditation, prayer, and spiritual ceremony. You are inspired to become an artist, teacher, leader, or organizer of humanitarian service, either as a priest or spiritual adviser. The word *saint* is a word that carries the number 9 frequency. It is a feminine or masculine number.

11

This is the number of the wounded healer, and your guidance is here to walk you through the dark night of the soul, so you know that you are not alone. You will be assisted to overcome and learn important lessons from all your hardships. Enlightenment, self-discovery, and psychic abilities open after you pass through the light at the end of the tunnel. Intuition becomes heightened and prepares you to unfold gifts as a healer and a messenger through various means of creative talents. Your connection to a higher source is a protecting force on your soul-life journey, and you feel that an anomaly of energy pulsing through you at various times in life, sometimes slowly but always purposely, is directing you toward specific goals. When you reach the treasure at the end your expedition, you welcome this frequency as a magical companion who understands you like no other. It is a masculine and feminine energy.

22

This guidance is the mover and shaker of all our numbers. It has all the qualities of the number 11 plus a push toward self-motivation, serving as a bonfire to get things really moving in your life. This is the frequency of the master builder, and it is here to assist you in accomplishing big things. It calls on you to create, endure, and complete tasks that seem nearly impossible. This companion nudges you forward in all your efforts and brings together the components necessary to accomplish any impervious endeavors. It is the energy of spiritual strength and courage and stops at nothing to help you build a better world for all of us to live in. It is a masculine number.

33

Your guidance leads you into healing through spiritual vision and creative outlets. Thirty-three is the number of the master teachers of our time and the time before. Yours is the path of divine expression through the power of the spoken word (communication). The master number 33 guides, heals, directs, and restores people with its altruistic powers and rather high energy. You are guided to discipline your sensitivity and direct it toward self-compassion. Your empathy is a gift that has no limits when expressing your truth backed by the healing love of your inner guidance. Self-expression must be inspired by the fruits of your imagination, touched by spirit, and then shared with the outside world. You are here to teach, heal, and lead humankind to a higher state of awareness. It is a feminine number.

44

The superpower of the master number 44 is in enterprise and business toward the path of sacred order. You have the ability to attract resources in perfect harmony with nature and our environment. I envision you as a pure electrical current of energy balancing commodities in the perfect flow of giving and receiving. This guide combines the strengths of the master numbers 11, 22, and 33. Not only do they foresee and implement what is needed to create something monumental; they want that bigger picture to help humankind in an enormous way. They are insightful like the 11, creative like the 22, nurturing like the 33, and they advise you to refuse to be intimidated by any challenges along your path. They help you to be hardworking, disciplined, systematic, professional, trustworthy, and composed physically, mentally, and spiritually. They are deeply spiritual, wise, and inspirational to many people. You are here to help yourself and others advance to the next level of incarnation. When working with this guide, you have the power of dream materialization and can break the chains of the material world by lifting the veils to see reality. This number is the vibration of self- discipline, abundance, and success through balance. Balancing between two worlds in the areas of family/work, spirit/earth, and emotions/ logic, 44s need to build a strong foundation in all of them. Balancing issues come up around the number 8, and the number 44 is about business building and how it can be related to benefit present and future generations.

<u>CHAPTER 21</u>

Cycle Numbers

Everything involving numbers starts and ends with the zero. Within the zero, we have the absolute infinity of wholeness available to us, and although it is beyond time and space, the closest we can imagine being present within this circle would be a feeling of love. The fifth dimension is a state of love and light that some would refer to as nirvana. This is our natural state of being, without the concept of time and space. I believe that we all were originally born out of the center of the zero and decided to experience life through the frequencies of our birth dates and names. This is where numbers come in, because each number has its own frequency, with defining qualities, personalities, and characteristics, but we all were meant to ascend back to the zero at the end of our journeys, and for some of us, it has taken many lifetimes. Therefore, Egyptian numerology is so important because it navigates our souls to our highest vibrations and allows us a clear path back home—and back to the alpha and omega, which is the essence of Divine Energy.

Using numbers, we were able to create time to guide us into seasons, months, and eventually hours of the day. Time was a tool we used to help navigate through the seasons of our lives, but somewhere along the line, we became overtaken with time and forgot its origin. We have allowed time to control us instead of guide us. The fear that time produces is directly connected to our nervous systems and only when we release it do we center ourselves back into the state of nirvana, or the fifth-dimensional state of being. Therefore, meditation, self-reflection, and silence have become popular and essential.

Just in case we forgot where we came from, we used numbers and their frequencies to trigger awakenings within our psyches. This is where cycles come in. They are important marks in time, keeping us on track with our soul-life paths, purposes, and destinies. Along with the planets, time has become a unique tool for us to understand and follow. If you are interested in exploring the definition of your life journey and allowing a refreshing perspective to flow forth like a river or stream of invigorating awareness, I recommend opening your eyes to the functions of our cycles. We created cycles within cycles, and each has a significant meaning and timeline that includes specific states of awareness that each of us can relate to.

There are cycles within cycles because the universe loves her cycles. We have season cycles, number cycles, color cycles (rainbow), sound cycles (musical scales), moon cycles, developmental cycles, chronological cycles, and so on. Everything is connected, and every cycle has a spiritual meaning within its momentum, no matter what it is. Each cycle has a numeric frequency that is used as a guideline, and it all began with zero.

Understanding our own personal cycles and how they operate in our lives is only the beginning to building a bridge of alignment with our soul-life agreements. When I was able to put the pieces of the puzzle together by following the meaning of my life cycles, I became empowered with a force of action to forge forward and onward to complete my soul-life journey with a newfound dedication and clarity. If you want to learn more about the cycles of your life and how they tie into the reason you came to this planet at this time in our universe, you can use the following guidelines to help you map out the course of your life.

Saturn Cycles

The Saturn return is a cycle we all experience around the age of twenty-eight, and it usually lasts anywhere from two to five years. This cycle occurs in our lives every twenty-nine years, as Saturn literally returns to the same position in our solar system as when we were born. Even though Saturn's complete cycle around the sun takes approximately twenty-nine years, the hard aspect of transiting Saturn to its place in your birth chart has squares and oppositions that take place every seven years. Each seven-year period ends with a new phase of maturing and taking inventory of our lives, thus the phrase *seven-year itch.*

The characteristics of Saturn are associated with being a teacher who concerns itself with karma and the lessons that past experiences might bring. Its energy serves as a catalyst to motivate us to move forward in our lives. It is a masculine energy and rules both Capricorn and Aquarius, the tenth and eleventh houses. Saturn signifies the boundaries of personal awareness and experience. Everything that arises from its influence carries the aim of creating firmer foundations for future potential. It is impacted holding the ouroboros, the serpent who eats its own tail, a symbol of eternal regeneration that forges birth and death into the endless cycle of past, present, and future.

The Saturn return has attracted an unfairly bad reputation, commonly labeled as a difficult and challenging time. The Saturn archetype reflects the boundary between the conscious awareness of one's self and the unconscious. This part of the cycle asks that we examine the self at a deep and personal level. The way we approach this powerful cycle can make an enormous difference to our experiences because it can be an extremely challenging period or an amazing rewarding time of self-discovery.

It is all about reconnecting with the laws of nature on a profound level. The natural planetary cycles are part of this process; these cycles of maturation are an intrinsic part of our spiritual growth, and with the awareness of what they reflect to us in our lives, we can align our egos with the intentions of our souls and take full advantage of the energetic opportunities being offered to us.

I have decided to focus first on the seven-year cycle because it happens most frequently and eventually includes all the other life cycles as we follow it through a hundred-year life span. The most important years are when they all meet and intersect with one another. I have listed the cycles that merge along with the seven-year cycle, including the Saturn return.

Cycle Years in Egyptian Numerology

Number 7—Cycle years—Maturation triggers

Number 9—Cycle years—Completion triggers

Number 12—Cycle years—Portals of transportation

Number 28—Cycle years—Transformation—Saturn return

Cycle Number 7

The seven-year cycle occurs most frequently and symbolizes the seeker, thinker, and searcher of truth, but it plays an important role in our daily lives as a mark in time. The universe uses time to illustrate events, circumstances, and occurrences by evaluating the frequency and delivering its value within a series of years. This means different things for everyone, but we all experience these transitions during these cycles. They are markers in time that we use to evaluate the production of our lives.

First Seven-Year Cycle (Ages 0–7)—the Transition Years

We notice that we were born into specific families, locations, and spiritual or religious preference. The first seven years are the adjustment years. This is where we get used to the material world and geographical surroundings and our belief systems begin to form.

Many of us incarnate with memories of our past lives. This can range from familiarity with family members and clothing styles during dress-up to continuous dreams or repeating nightmares. We often converse with invisible friends from the other side who are very real to us but who do not appear to anyone else. Childhood illnesses may develop but later disappear as we get older.

We develop coping skills that will later break or make us. We also decide currently whether we feel safe in the world and get our sense of self through the eyes of our parents and family members. We are in cocoons or bubbles of light where angels frequently visit.

At around the age of seven, we have lost our baby teeth, and according to researchers, our bodies replace themselves with largely new sets of cells every seven to ten years.

Second Seven-Year Cycle (Ages 7–14)—the DevelopingYears, Influenced by Cycles 7, 9, and 12

We develop physically through a hormonal maturation determining our reproductive cycles. Our stress levels from the first seven years can alter this process if the stress was extreme. Rest assured that all this is predetermined in the akashic records before birth.

Emotionally, we develop in the social arena. We are introduced to friends and search out comfort levels in the outside world. Some children prefer to be alone, finding solace still in the angelic realm.

Intellectually, we are challenged in school. A problem can occur for those of us who have not developed a trust in the outside world. It is nearly impossible to open the learning mind when the emotional self will not go forward. Mental stimulation simply gets short-circuited when our emotions are not at peace.

We start developing our own interests, and sometimes this causes us to butt heads with family members over plans or expectations. Our behavior can become erratic as the will of us children combats the will of the adults. We are not seen or considered individuals yet with the right to make up our own minds. A compromise must intervene, or struggles will prevail, and this is a promise. The portal to creativity opens at this time, and we are introduced to our talents, whether they are forced on us or self-inspired. Our creative purpose is announced to us in one way or another. Invisible friends may disappear, but we will be connected to Spirit through our creative gifts.

Spiritually, we are assigned inner guidance through a confirmation of faith. This is done in the Catholic religion, Jewish tradition, Native American tradition, and others. If we are not assigned a religion, this is also part of our divine plan. The magical portal opens during this cycle, and the path into the astral plane can become a common occurrence, especially during sleep and dreams. Regardless of our religion, we will intuitively know what path is spiritually the right one for us.

I started to have dream premonitions and astral travel at age fourteen. Our psychic abilities come alive and slowly introduce themselves to us if we are open to receive them. I was able to read people's energy by holding their hands, and I could tell things about them that I could not have known. I started receiving memories of past-life experiences, and even though I was raised a Catholic, as I mentioned earlier on in the book, I started calling myself an *extended Catholic* because Catholicism had never prepared me for these psychic adventures. I started reading Eastern philosophy because I just did not fit into the classification of my religion any longer. My parents were confused, and to be honest, so was I.

On a karmic note, our whole world can change at this time. It is now that the universe unfolds to us our first and probably biggest life lesson. Generally speaking, between the ages of twelve and fourteen, a huge event takes place, changing the course of our lives forever. This could be in the form of an illness, new member of the family, parental divorce, a move in location, death in the family, abuse, or a loss of great magnitude. Whatever it is, it will give birth to the lessons we are meant to learn in this lifetime and be the driving force moving us in the direction of our soul-life purposes and toward emotional maturation. It most likely will rock our world on all levels; physically, emotionally, mentally, socially, and spiritually. At this time, it appears devastating, but at the end our life cycle, we will be the most grateful for it.

Third Seven-Year Cycle (Ages 14–21)—the Formable Years

Our social role in society has been established by now. We either are social rock stars or have settled into being recluses. We are anticipating our futures and deciding how we are going to fit into this vast unexplored world. All of life's components have been introduced, and we must accept our position or struggle.

We are physically developed and continue to make minor physical adjustments during this time. Emotionally, we have learned how to manipulate our surroundings to get what we want. At this time, we can easily fall into dangerous illusions. We can become overconfident in the illusion of the material world and believe that it is all life has to offer. We become eager to strike out into the world to master it our way, but we are not quite mature enough to see the dangers lurking around us. So it is.

We start experimenting with the freedom of becoming sovereign entities in relationships and education and possibly live away from home for the first time. Dependency and independency become interchangeable until we are confident enough to let go of our parents' lead ropes. All this uncertainty takes precedence above everything else happening in our lives. We start making our own decisions with consequences, and life truly begins.

Fourth Seven-Year Cycle (Ages 21–28)— the Transformation Years, Influenced by All Cycles, 7, 9, 12, and 28

These are called the transformational years, but I refer to them as the *invincible years*. We are alive and thriving in the world in all areas of our lives. The idea of reaching for the stars is possible, and we have our whole futures ahead of us. Life appears uncertain at times, but we are too busy to pay much attention to fear.

Some people say that we end our childhoods and become adults during this cycle, but it is not until we reach the age of twenty-eight that we begin adulthood.

Some of us choose to get married, go to college, start careers, have children, travel, or relocate from our family homelands. No matter what we decide to do, the karmic paths we encounter between the ages of twenty-six and twenty-eight will surface and make some much-needed adjustments to our lives. It is called the Saturn return. Everything we do before the age of twenty-eight is in preparation for our soul-life paths. This is much like the life-altering change that happened to us between the ages of twelve and fourteen—but bigger. Our Saturn returns meet with all life cycles (7, 9, 12, and 28) and have the power to transform our lives on all levels, pushing us into the right directions. If met with resistance, we become depressed, lost, and unhappy. Many people attest to experiencing the undercurrents of this cycle years before it hits. They report feeling the earth moving underneath their feet, and it makes them feel uneasy because they intuitively know that something big is going to happen but are not quite sure what it is.

For me, it was the birth of my daughter, which led me to starting my own childcare business. I had no idea that I was going to do this, and years before my twenty-eighth birthday, I could feel that my life was going to change without a clue as to what it would look like. I did not resist the changes. Instead, I went with the miracles that life was showing me, and sure enough, it was grandeur than I could have ever dreamed possible.

We must trust the universe because it will deliver. This is the time when all our illusions are brought to our attention in order to open us to the truth. If we follow the paths of our hearts, we are set free from the fears we are holding on to. We must allow the universe to shape and guide us into the directions we were designed to travel and hold on to our seats because the ride will take us places beyond our wildest dreams. We will be transformed!

Fifth Seven-Year Cycle (Ages 28–35)—the Productive Years

We are still in the grip of the transformative years, and this could take another seven years to develop, depending on where our life-path directions take us. The productive years find us in construction of our new lives. We could be starting new careers, having children, or goingback to school.

We are building foundations for the rest of our lives, so we take it easy and enjoy the ride. Our health is stable if we continue to be mindful of exercising and maintaining a well-balanced diet. Many of us find that our bodies change during this cycle. We no longer can eat the way we did when we were in our twenties. The invincible illusion starts to wane, and we realize we have limits that we need to abide by. This is normal.

Socially, we may lose touch with friends who were once stimulating in previous years and become acquainted with friends who share our newfound interests. We find promising purposes in our lives, and it can be exciting as our new fields of interest change and develop. Emotionally, we are lifted by deeper relationships and start to define the true meaning of friendship and love. We realize we must continue to feed our souls, and finding, building, and maintaining balance in our lives becomes a sacred dance.

Sixth Seven-Year Cycle (Ages 35–42)—the Settling Years

We have been busy getting our careers and families off the ground. A lot of the previous years were focused on other people, places, and things. This cycle is about maintaining our balance in the multiphases of our lives. We can now sit back and take inventory of our progress. We make time to reflect and inspect our relationships, occupations, locations, and spiritual progress.

Our physical bodies are changing, and we may be experiencing limitations we didn't anticipate or expect. Adjustments are made to accommodate our lifestyles, and a gust of wind may blow through our hormones, asking whether we would like the last chance to have children or start families if we have not already done so.

Spiritually, we question our life paths, and any adjustments needed to be made might have brought up some serious life challenges. Being attracted to strengthen our connection to Higher Source is common during this term. While men are challenged in the stamina department, women start experiencing the divine feminine, and changes are made to bring forward the feminine aspects of our lives. For both men and women, a balance of the yin and yang is part of the developing nature.

Seventh Seven-Year Cycle (Ages 42–49)—the Sovereign Years, Influenced by Cycles 7, 9, and 12

The previous settling cycle brought to our attention that maturity has taken place, and the invincible stage we experienced in our twenties has all but faded. We now find ourselves grounded and established in the maturity of our lives, and it is time to look at ourselves internally and discover who we are without the outside world to define us.

If our parents are still living, we are most likely being of service to them in their elderly years. Between our taking care of our children and our parents, life can become quite an emotional roller coaster ride. Solitude and meditation are needed but often take a back seat to our busy, hectic lives.

We are pulled in several directions all at once, and life becomes overwhelming. Anxiety, depression, and addiction often surface during this cycle as we struggle to find solace in an engaging and complicated world. Exercising, eating a healthy diet, and practicing daily meditation are put on the top of our priority list as we search ourselves, our identities, for a richer meaning in life. We find the need to stop identifying ourselves by what we do in the world; we begin to focus on the fact that we are human beings, not human doings. We also decide whether we are living toward our life purposes or just making a means to put food on the table, and if the latter is true, we get honest and ask ourselves how we can make life more substantial.

Many love relationships begin or end during this cycle, especially after we take a rigorous inventory of the progress in our lives. We may search for deeper meaning and discover we need to either be alone at this point of our journeys or join new partnerships with those we believe will add the missing pieces to our puzzles. Regardless of what we do, our emotional, mental, and spiritual states will reflect our progress and direct us on the path toward our destinies.

Eighth Seven-Year Cycle (Ages 49–56)—the Cleansing Years, Influenced by Cycles 7, 9, and 28

It is at this point that we realize we have lived half our lives. Women go through the stages of menopause, and men go through the stages of andropause. Women's reproductive cycles come to an end, and women take time to define themselves as women and not just mothers, potential mothers, or sex objects. Oftentimes, while a woman's emotional body is readjusting to the hormonal fluctuation, it is necessary for her to put up a temporary wall toward men until her body, heart, mind, and spirit realign, and this is why it is called men-o-pause. She needs to identify herself as a woman of power, strength, and vitality during this crucial time in her life.

Men, on the other hand, go through andropause, which is the declination of the male hormone testosterone. Although men's physical symptoms appear less severe than women's, this change is taking place and recognizable by many symptoms. Besides the physical symptoms, men often get an inner drive to reorganize things. This is their spring-cleaning in life. While stepping into their maturity, they might clean out the garage, storage, closets, cars, or boats and throw out the things that no longer serve them. No longer identifying as boys with excuses, they are going through a transformation at this stage. What was commonly seen as the midlife crisis is now a midlife opportunity. The paternal myth that men cheat and have affairs is no longer acceptable. Men are evolving spiritually and no longer tolerate being driven by their sexual infatuations. They hold themselves up to a higher standard and take responsibility for their cosmic evolution. While women are reorganizing on the inside, men are cleaning up on the outside. This is the yin-and-yang balance taking form.

Ninth Seven-Year Cycle (Ages 56–63)—the Harvest Years, Influenced by Cycles 7, 9, 12, and 28

Here we go again; the second Saturn return comes around. We probably felt the engine revving up a couple of years prior and have begun to make room for the major events to enter during this stage of transformation. By now, we are aware of how successful the first Saturn return was, and the universe has probably handed us clues as to what is expected of us.

These are the beginning of our harvest years, and as in every harvest, we will reap what we have sown. Our higher selves guide us toward our destinies, and being aware of this truth makes the introduction easier. It is an exciting time, but if for some reason we resist, it wreaks havoc in our lives in the form of physical illness, depression, or anxiety. We have the immense power of all the cycles behind this one, so we must be mindful and aware enough to use this time wisely to deliver our best efforts.

In chapter 22 in this book, there is a section on the harvest years, or the golden goal years. It explains how to calculate and utilize these years through Egyptian numerology.

Tenth Seven-Year Cycle (Ages 63–70)—the Bucket List Years

If we have made bucket lists, this is the time to review them. We have several years to complete our lists, but we want to get started while we have the health and money to achieve our goals. We usually look toward retirement from our careers during this cycle. We have most likely worked for several years, and now is the time to slow down and enjoy life to its fullest.

If we do not have bucket lists, this is the time to start them. We can use our imaginations, and the sky is the limit. We can start by writing down all the things we are interested in but have not had the time to complete. Once we activate our higher selves, we ask Spirit for guidance. If we are not interested in making bucket lists, we can direct our focus on what makes us happy. Remember—we cannot take our time or money with us, so we might as well spend it doing something we love.

Eleventh Seven-Year Cycle (Ages 70–77)—the Serenity Years, Influenced by Cycles 7, 9, and 12

These are the years to gather up our momentum and direct our wisdom outwardly. We have now learned that it does not pay to worry about things we cannot do anything about. We volunteer our time and energy to people, places, and things that interest and need us. We have so much to offer the world, and during this cycle, our wisdom is needed everywhere. If we have grandchildren, it is a wonderful period to spend time with them. We can help our adult children by making a regular schedule to teach the grandchildren who we are and what we know.

We have gained an understanding of life that is immensely valuable and priceless, and it is imperative we allow it to be accessible to others. This can be in the form of writing, teaching, or creating memoirs. The serenity years offer us the opportunity to go within and prepare statements of our lives to deliver to the outside world. So many people believe that life is wasted on the youth, but it does not have to be. At a time in the world when seniors are not visible, we must make a stand and be seen. We are making a comeback in society as others welcome us wise ones into the circle.

We do not stop playing because we are old; we become old because we stop playing. There are only four secrets to staying young, being happy, and achieving success. You must laugh and find humor every day.

You've got to have dreams. When you lose your dreams, you die.

We have so many people walking around asleep and don't even know it! There is a huge difference between growing older and growing up.

If you are nineteen years old and lie in bed for one full year and don't do one constructive thing, you will turn twenty years old.

If I am eighty-six years old and stay in bed for a year and never do anything, I will turn eighty-seven.

Anybody can grow older. That doesn't take a special gift or ability. The intention is to mature by always finding opportunity in change.

Have no regrets.

The elderly usually have remorse not for what we did but rather for things we never did. The only people who dread death are those with regrets.

Twelfth Seven-Year Cycle (Ages 77–84)—the Magical Years, Influenced by Cycles 7, 9, 12, and 28

The third and final Saturn return for most of us takes place during this cycle. Many of us use this cycle to exit the dimension and planet. It is an individual journey, and we have the immense power of Saturn behind us to support whatever decisions we make during this time. Obligations usually wind down, and we put our end of life arrangements in order.

We carefully review our life experiences and find areas that need completion, closure, or order as we process our lives with the integrity we deserve. Making necessary adjustments to our financial situations so we allow ourselves the opportunity to settle down in comfortable surroundings is a luxury we look forward to. Friends and family are important to us during this cycle, and it is essential we communicate our needs and desires.

If we are fortunate enough to have animal companions, this bonding assists us emotionally. Spending time with children, given their candid nature, brings us much joy and purpose. As we enter the conclusions of our lives, we are closer to the realm of heaven, and both children and animals relate best to our state of being. We allow ourselves to become familiar with the other realms as we make our adjustments to the otherside and know that we will be back if needed—in the blink of an eye.

Nine-Year Cycle

Within the nine-year cycle, we learn that our feelings are the only means to advocate for personal freedom. The ninth year is of endings and conclusions, offering us a chance to free ourselves of the misguided beliefs that have *always* caused unhappiness, boredom, dissatisfaction, and stagnation. The ninth year teaches us how to break free from the past by surrendering our grasp on it, and without this awareness, we will forever be victims of something that once happened to us. It is now time to heal.

Nothing new happens in the nine-year cycle until the unavoidable endings take place, and the more we seek to begin something new without first freeing the old, the more resistance the universe sends our way. If we do not try to accept our emotional realities, we find that our histories repeat themselves in the following nine years.

The ninth year asks us to reflect on our lives' continuous journeys and contemplate everything that has happened to us. There will be circumstances that we do not want to remember, and these are memories we are blocking from our consciousness. These are the very incidents and situations needing to be addressed, and they act as heavy loads, weighing us down like anchors, preventing our forward momentum. The more genuine *intent* we use to allow forgotten memories to resurface, the easier it becomes to adopt the nine year's healing process.

It is the sheer weight of avoiding past and present emotion that causes depression, even though we try to fool ourselves into believing that we can escape depression by deflecting these emotions. This pretense creates a deeper denial and, eventually, deeper despondency. If we find ourselves focused on anger, regret, fear, or grief to the extent that we cannot live constructively, there is a good chance we are using these emotions as excuses for continuing to deny other emotions that are even more deeply buried. Denial is no longer a privilege on this earth. It is denial that causes many of the dire problems humanity faces today, and this applies as much to our personal lives as it does to life in general.

Being afraid to own our feelings is a natural response, and like all feelings, they must follow their own evolutionary processes and be allowed to *move*. When we cling to fear, we are refusing its ability to support us, and by preventing its movement, we become paralyzed by it. The natural progression is to allow ourselves to feel our fear, accept its presence, and allow it to move through and out of us. This process promotes courage and growth—the ability to recognize those things to be feared and those that need not be feared at all. Honoring our feelings as extensions of our senses, intuitions, and instincts is vital to our survival.

Being honest with ourselves is crucial in this process because mere positive thinking can do more harm than good, because if our thoughts and feelings are not in alignment, we create stagnant energy. Our thoughts and feelings are two different forces that need to be experienced separately so that we can tell them apart. When our masculine thoughts and feminine feelings find peace and join forces, our personal power to survive and prosper increases significantly and our entire beings evolve.

The ninth year drags us backward in what appears to be the wrong direction, but this guidance is necessary so that we find the unfinished issues preventing us from going forward. It is essential for this term to be an emotional ride. We are in a cycle of assessing past emotions, along with assimilating new emotional situations in the present, which in part trigger the old feelings needing to be released.

The circumstances we encounter are reenactments of the past, in different forms, representing the consequences of actions, inaction, beliefs, and attitudes. We cannot live fully in the present if parts of us are stuck in the past. Therefore, we want to go back and retrieve the lost parts of ourselves that have been unresolved and cemented in our subconscious.

Generosity, kindness, and compassion play important roles in this course of development, and through a greater depth of understanding of ourselves, we become sympathetic to other people's realities and aware of how we are all compounding certain problems by denying the feelings involved. We become aware of the difference between compassion and guilt.

Currently, if we are reluctantly involved in something, guilt may have convinced us that it is the right thing to do—and maybe it is. Maybe it isn't. The only way for us to be sure is by trusting our intuitions to guide us, and it is in the ninth year that we realize the extent to which guilt keeps us from achieving happiness and how much we have denied guilt by reversing it into blame.

Uncomfortable memories arise to be healed, allowing us to create more inner space for happiness to surface, and inaccurate beliefs become replaced by new truths, perspectives, and potentials. As we accept what *has* happened to us, we develop luminous visions of what we *want to* generate in our lives, and we transform the old selves into the present selves, allowing our will and desires to determine a whole new future.

Not all endings are connected to tumultuous emotions. Some situations are finally concluded, bringing much reprieve. We must not assume the worst. We must accept that our pasts are the ground we had to cover to get where we desired to be, and our understanding of our journeys manifests the nine-year cycle into the most exhilarating and dynamic pilgrimages we will ever travel.

The chart that follows symbolizes the completion or ending of aspects or events of our lives that can be identified during the nine-year cycle:

Age 9—Completion of childhood
Age 18—Completion of self-awareness
Age 27—Completion of adolescence
Age 36—Completion of invincibility
Age 45—Completion of ego identification
Age 54—Completion of reproduction
Age 63—Completion of careers
Age 72—Completion of resistance
Age 81—Completion of material world

<u>CHAPTER 22</u>

Transformative Years

Twenty-Eight-Year Cycles

Within the nine-year cycles are the transformative cycles. They last twenty-seven years or more. The minimum time span is always at least three full cycles of nine years, but they can last longer and up to thirty-five years. These coincide with our Saturn-return cycles, so I call them our *transformative cycles*. The transformative cycles form the base structure of all the cycles found in one's chart, including the life path, pinnacles, challenges, and medium-term and the short-term cycles. The transformative cycles describe the three great divisions of our lives: (1) opening, (2) dynamic, and (3) golden.

First Cycle

This opening cycle begins at birth and ends at the dynamic cycle. This period finds us discovering our true nature within the powerful forces present in our environments, families, and socioeconomic conditions. It lays the groundwork for the individuation process. It contains the favorable and constructive circumstances that build our character, personalities, strengths, and positive programming, which becomes the foundation for our success and happiness.

The numerical vibrations of our opening cycles are simply the sum of the digits making up our birth months. Most of us will not even need to reduce these, apart from those of us born in October, November, and December.

Those of us born in September will have the number 9 as our opening-cycle number and will experience this vibrational pattern during our first cycles.

Those of us born in December have the number 3 as our opening- cycle number because December is the twelfth month of our calendar year (12 = 1 + 2 = 3) and will experiences this vibrational pattern during our first cycle.

* Those of us born in November are considered to have opening cycles of 2 because the master number 11 is too difficult a vibration for young people to express, at least until our later teenage years or early twenties.

Second Cycle

This cycle is always set in motion during the transformative period.

Currently, we follow the emergence of our individual and creative talents. The initial part of this cycle finds us in the early and mid-thirties, representing our individuality and determination to find our true place in this world, while the early forties and fifties allow us a greater degree of self-mastery and influence over our environments.

The dynamic cycle represents our passions, interests, and work in the world, most commonly pertaining to careers and the focus of our adult lives. It is the period when the vibrations of our birthdays and birth month numbers are expressed the strongest and is the time frame when we have the potential to manifest particular gifts, talents, or long- held dreams.

It represents our greatest achievements and the contributions we make to ourselves and the lives of others, whether for the good or not so good. It describes the nature of our legacies and how our presence forges a lasting change in our world.

Our dynamic numbers have been a driving force in our lives ever since we took our first breath of air, and they continue to mature throughout our lifetimes. Like all the numbers, dynamic numbers' potency is contingent on our energy levels. The higher we vibrate, the stronger the number works for us, and the gifts and talents of this number continue to bear fruit and support us. If our energy levels are low, the number continues to challenge us and serves as a reminder for us to up our game. All our challenges are opportunities for growth, so the lower our frequencies, the more challenges we encounter. This is a universal law, and it plays out beautifully in the vibrational dance of numbers.

The numerical vibration of the dynamic cycle, or second cycle, is determined by the sum of our birthdays and birth months, which is the sum of the digits of the day and the month on which we were born.

Those of us born on November 7 will have the number 9 as our dynamic-cycle number and will experience this vibrational pattern during this term. November is the eleventh month of our calendar year, added to the seventh day of the month (11 + 7 = 18 = 1 + 8 = 9).

We must always reduce to a single-digit number unless it is a master number—11, 22, or 33.

The dynamic cycle of our lives begins during the number 1 personal year closest to our twenty-eight birthdays. For some of us, the number 1 personal year will fall before our twenty-eighth birthday. In this case, the beginning of the dynamic cycle is not felt until the twenty-eighth birthday, although events corresponding to the upcoming cycle is set in motion during the transformative period.

Note that your birth personal year number is the same as your soul-life path number. To calculate your birth personal year or soul-life path number, add your birthday, month, and birth years, and reduce the sum to a single-digit number. If you were born on January 10, 2001 (1 + 1+ 2 + 1 = 5), your birth personal year number or soul-life path number is number 5.

The Third

The golden cycle is the time in our lives when we finally arrive at what is termed our *golden years* and sometimes referred to as our harvest years. Saturn has completed the second twenty-nine-year orbit journey around the sun, and we come into our second Saturn return around the age of fifty-eight, although the shift of energy can be felt at a much younger age. This energy creates a momentum until our third Saturn return, which occurs in our mid-eighties. While this can be a challenging period requiring big changes in work, relationships, and other areas of our lives, the second is typically less tumultuous than the first. Saturn is known as the "Lord of Karma" or the "Lord of Harvest."

It is a time when we reap what we sow and gather our dreams, passions, and aspirations and attempt to materialize them once and for all in this incarnation. These are called the quiet years of reflection and meditation. We have within us a wealth of knowledge and experience emerging to fruition and calling us to pass this wisdom onto future generations. It is a time of gathering and planting our innermost encouragements while finding creative ways to deliver their meanings.

This is the frequency we serve in our later years and where we get our second wind in life, demonstrating noble attempts in completing or accomplishing the items on our bucket lists. The best part about this term is that we are supplied with an incredible amount of experience and knowledge, which we have acquired from our previous years.

Right when we thought we were going to retire and take it easy, a stream of inspiration floods our consciousness, and we begin industrious attempts in making our special dreams come true. We intuitively know what we want or need to get done to put the icing on the cake before we exit to the next dimension. This numeric frequency is calculated by adding our destiny and path numbers. It delivers the message of what we are meant to do in our golden-cycle years.

We use the power of these forces to guide us to our final deliverance of productivity. This is a popular time when individuals contact me for a reading and guidance on how to align with their soul-life agreements. For some reason, people think that they are too old to pursue their dreams, when in reality, it is the perfect time to get started because it is at this time when we have the most knowledge and experience to offer the world. We accomplish in a small amount of time what would have taken us years when we were younger.

This cycle represents the flowering of our inner beings—our freedom to explore the progress of our true nature and deliver the fruit of our labor. It is during this cycle that we have the·greatest degree of self-expression and power. We may choose to share the wisdom we have gained by giving back to the world as teachers, writers, artists, or mentors.

Saturn return can be an extremely challenging or rewarding time. It brings a spiritual energy that requires us to go within, meditate, slow down, listen, and witness. It is here to help us understand that life's lessons are meant not to punish us but to help us learn. It asks us to open our minds and our hearts and stand face-to-face with who we truly are, including the good, bad, and ugly. It is the point at which we realize we have lived half our lives. Women and men go through the stages of menopause and andropause (refer to the eighth seven-year cycle). One of the most common regrets people voice at the end of their lives is that they did not honor their own truths and follow their hearts; rather, they lived in accordance with others' expectations. This is a rich opportunity for us to re-create our lives, having the most meaningful and vibrant remaining years, so that before we transition into the next dimension, we look back and know we lived through our lives with love and light. Sometimes we take up new careers, advance our education, or even experience our greatest achievements during this time of our lives.

In traditional numerology, these years are termed pinnacle, cycle, or period years, but in Egyptian numerology, we call them our harvest or golden-cycle years.

The final, or golden, cycle begins during the number 1 personal year closest to the fifty-seventh birthday. As with the dynamic cycle, if it falls before, the effect will not be felt until the fifty-seventh birthday, although events corresponding to it are set in motion during the transformative period. The golden cycle lasts for the remainder of our lifetimes.

The numerical vibrations of our golden cycle are determined by the sum of our soul-life path and destiny numbers.

It's important to note that the vibrational patterns of these three cycles are always reduced to single digits unless their sums are master number 11 or 22 (in fact, it's impossible for anyone to have an opening cycle number of 22 because there are only twelve months).

The ages that these cycles influence may vary from person to person based on the life-path numbers. Use your life-path number from the calculation explained previously and calculate your destiny number by referring to chapter 19, "Sacred Oracle Word." You can use the arithmancy calculator to get the total of your birth certificate name. The total is your destiny number. You can also refer to my first book, *Egyptian Numerology: Emergence into the Fifth Dimension*, which goes into more detail.

Use the following chart to calculate the ages of your cycle numbers based on your life-path number.

Your Life-Path Number	First-Cycle Years (Opening)	Second-Cycle Years (Dynamic)	Third-Cycle Years (Golden)
1	0–35	35–62	62–
2	0–34	34–61	61–
3	0–33	33–60	60–
4	0–32	32–59	59–
5	0–31	31–58	58–
6	0–30	30–57	57–
7	0–29	29–56	56–
8	0–28	28–55	55–
9	0–27	27–54	54–
11	0–34	34–61	61–
22	0–32	32–59	59–

Because Egyptian numerology uses astrology, I am including the elements of earth, air, water, and fire to assist in the definition within the first cycle.

Month	Cycle Number	Element
January	1	earth
February	2	air
March	3	water
April	4	fire
May	5	earth
June	6	air
July	7	water
August	8	fire
September	9	earth
October	1	air
November	2	water
December	3	fire

Characteristics of Elements

Earth: January—1, May—5, and September—9

grounded, trustworthy, ambitious, creative, social, kind, strong, perfectionist, industrious, practical, conservative, and sensual

Earth signs are primarily here to ground, center, and trust. You can find them living in the moment, trying to make the most out of life. They like things simple and are goal oriented and very practical people. Their grounded values are reliable, and they are real, authentic, straightforward people who believe in working hard and proving themselves. Actions speak louder than words to them, and they often detect things that go unnoticed to others.

Air: February—2, June—6, and October—1

communicative, clever, fair, spontaneous, philosophical, deep thinkers, intelligent, free spirited, logical, and idealistic

Air signs are capable of pure thought, imagination, and channeling spirit. They are free thinkers and love to communicate their visions. We find them in the fields of writing, teaching, and philosophy because they need to share their thoughts with the world. They can be unpredictable and spontaneous, expressing the element of surprise when you least expect it. They are social and feel content expressing themselves because they are comfortable in their own skin. Their interests reveal them to be bookworms, researchers, and intellectuals who love traveling and exploring. Their confidence can be misinterpreted as cockiness, but they are idealistic and enjoy the nicer things life has to offer.

Water: March—3, July—7, and November—2

emotional, empathic, receptive, deep feeling, romantic, intuitive, impulsive, private, sensitive, mysterious, artistic, and imaginative

Water signs show us the natural flow of resources, cleansing techniques, and how to feel our emotions on a deep level. They are highly aware, psychic, and empathic beings, allowing intuition to lead most of their decision-making. They are natural caregivers who seek to uplift others, but they are private and discreet about their own feelings. They imagine a completely different world and, through creative efforts, bring this world to life.

Fire: April—4, August—8, and December—3

enthusiastic, expressive, curious, compassionate, optimistic, independent, dramatic, high energy, enlightenment seeking, and impatient

Fire signs carry the passion to purify or destroy. They show us how to create and spark innate abilities and talents. They love having their own space and feeling a sense of freedom. Their fun, exciting, friendly, and encouraging nature affords them the opportunity to be inspirational and devoted people. They handle obstacles with a direct, head-on approach and are trailblazers who create opportunities for others. They cover up their emotions with dynamic strength and open to only a chosen few.

Opening Cycle: Number 1 (January and October)

Early in life, we find you strong, healthy, energetic, and independent. Solitude is satisfying because it affords you focus for projects. You enjoy socializing and sharing ideas with others, and your enthusiasm dictates leadership positions.

You are not an emotional person, and you lean toward being the logical thinker within your romantic relationships. Your emotions rarely swing high or low because you prefer to be stable, strong, sturdy, grounded, and solid. You understand practical relationships marked by common interests. Recognizing trust in yourself and others cultivates qualities of honesty and loyalty that are so important to you.

Your spiritual connections can be found in nature because acknowledging the intricate values that science has to offer is one of your greatest interests. You have a passionate creative side, blended with a vivid imagination, which needs exploration and release for you to maintain a healthy balance. You are superb when working with your hands, and you understand mathematics and music on a deep level.

Most likely, you find a job and stay with it for an extensive period until you decide on a life career. Experiencing a lot of short-term relationships does not appeal to you, as you prefer to be alone until the right person comes along. Being uniquely elegant, classy, and compassionate in mannerism, you do not bother with multiple emotional affairs but rather settle into a comfortable long-term partnership.

You are an independent soul who naturally moves out of the family home as soon as you can afford it, unless it offers you sanctuary to your preferred lifestyle. Having physical disciplines and testing your strength and vitality are part of your daily routine, and you desire to be healthy because understanding what is needed to maintain fitness comes naturally to you.

You are a pure soul with a heart of gold, a genuine, loyal, fiercely ambitious person who takes responsibility seriously, and this finds you sought after as a team player.

This is a cycle of much intensity because it forces you to use every one of your talents to achieve personal individuality, individuation, and independence. This is a cycle of integrating and focusing on your life's dream. Even though you will be tested, resources are available to you to overcome any obstacles and emerge from this cycle all the stronger. It requires determination, resilience, and strength, but all these characteristics become an integral part of your growing personality.

Dynamic Cycle: Number 1

You are nothing less than a force of nature. Original ideas flow through your mind when you are inspired, and elements gravitate seemingly out of nowhere to support your efforts. Strength of character follows you everywhere, and your leadership qualities are always gifts to be admired. People are attracted to your vivacious energy, trust your intuition, and follow when you are on fire and passionate about your projects.

Being a natural conduit with a direct line to Divine Source, you find that your soul is linked to Higher Spirit when you are clear and open. The number 1 creates a quickening and is a conduit between spirit and matter. It is the frequency representing alignment, and things happen quickly when you receive, listen to, and act on the intuitive insights that are given from Spirit. The number 1 dynamic cycle improves quality of life, attracts prosperity, nurtures relationships, builds careers, and accelerates spiritual growth with its dynamic force of nature.

The number 1 is a direct line from earth to sky, making a clear conduit or channel for focus, awareness, intuition, creativity, and independence. Your expression is forming your individuality and personal attainment in this lifetime. You learn to be strong, stand your ground, and are physically healthier and mentally stronger than most people. One can be a lonely number because of the self-sustenance and independent drive embedded deep in your DNA. Having creative inspiration and possessing enthusiasm and drive to accomplish a great many things, you are less lonely when sharing your knowledge, creativity, and interests with others. Your drive and potential for action come directly from the enormous depth of strength you have, and staying focused on your interests, not allowing yourself to be derailed or distracted, is one of your challenges.

You are gifted with a deep need to focus and pay attention to fine details, patterns, and synchronicities, which feeds your fascination in the fields of science, research, mathematics, music, art, and leadership. Ones are often blamed for having control issues, but actually, they focus so intensely on their interests that they just don't know how or when to let go.

The number 1 agreement finds combined creativity and confidence as an important expression vital to its path. Creativity and innovation require a willingness to be on the cutting edge of originality; this means being, acting, and often feeling different. Most 1's have intrinsically different ways of looking at and experiencing life and focusing on that which is unique. This quality manifests as early as infancy or as late as middle age.

You will create circumstances in your life that allow you opportunities to choose independence and self-sustenance to empower your life. You find your unique individuality and learn to self-express your divine nature freely. In this lifetime, you have set in motion the qualities of innovation, intuition, and self-awareness, and you must use these abilities to discipline yourself and teach others.

The summit-mountain path for this number is a joyful, passionate, and confident expression of personal magnetism, ingenuity, and productivity bordering on magic. Ones excel in any form of work involving some form of healing and creativity. At the highest levels, a 1 becomes a pure and nonresistant channel, a clear conduit through which an unlimited amount of creativity flows into and throughout the world.

Golden Cycle: Number 1

This number indicates you are destined to hold a position of leadership, and when you use your ability to think and act independently, living up to this standard comes naturally. By relying on determination, intuitive decisions, and strength, you make your own path during this term. Relying on your creativity and strength of character leads to success in new endeavors while you become a leader for others to follow.

It is time to pull out all the projects you have put on hold and become innovative, creative, and original through teaching, volunteering, instructing, or writing. You have accomplished many things in life that you can be proud of, and it is now time to pass this wisdom down to others.

Research topics that interest you, especially in areas where you contribute information to the benefit of others. Increase intuition and connection with Higher Source and get clear guidance on how to proceed in any area of your life, because it is time to focus on yourself and encourage strength, intelligence, intuition, and expression to take the front seat in your daily life. You will be active and may even begin a new career while manifesting your deepest desires.

Opening Cycle: Number 2 (February and November)

You are highly intuitive and acutely sensitive to your surroundings, possess the peacemaker gift, and have tremendous power through gentle persuasion. Because of your free-spirited nature and kind, compassionate disposition, we find you serving humanity from a young age.

You are creative, intuitive, and psychic, and you possess several artistic abilities. This is a wonderful release for your self-expression, and being an original thinker, as well as intelligent, spontaneous, and independent, makes you a magnet in social circles. You love people and have a gift toward understanding and compromise. When patience and flexibility are offered, there are no limits to your loving relationships.

Cooperation is a word associated with the vibration of this number. You are a master of duality and can see many sides of a single situation. This makes you an asset in a group arena where mediation, guidance, or psychic reading is concerned. The number 2 holds the seed of creativity. You create from a song that lingers deep within your heart, and though you are often blamed for idealism, you desire others to see their visions through your eyes of beauty. You enliven dreams, awaken the imagination, and balance the inner imagination with outer realities, making all aspects more appealing and beneficial. This number is about creating balance in your life between the yin and yang and with the five elements: (1) earth, (2) air, (3) water, (4) fire, and (5) ether.

Seek out beauty and harmonious environments, spend time in nature, and enjoy the peace of close companionship. Your goals in life are geared to adding harmony within all your activities.

The number 2 is here to learn how to overcome judgment and codependence, build confidence, and nurture a healthy self-esteem. It is the energy of relationships, creativity, romance, beauty, and balance.

Dynamic Cycle: Number 2

Equilibrium and balance are your natural forte. When walking into a room of people, you intuitively know the climate of energy just by tuning in through your senses. You automatically start forming the harmony process toward any imbalanced situation by performing your charm, grace, and beauty through whatever medium necessary to bring peace.

If you are mature enough in your skills of mindfulness and psychic talents, your calming essence is all that is necessary to bring order to a chaotic situation. Nothing remains off balance for long when you are present and vibrating at your highest energy level.

The number 2 is our hope in the world for beauty, balance, harmony, love, and peace. You are a natural at balancing polarities, which brings peace when opposites find symmetry. Because you are empathic, learning about your intuition, sensitivities, and psychic gifts and protecting your feelings are crucial and beneficial when you start at a young age. You are attracted to areas in life that need equilibrium because you naturally find a connection and synchronicity that offer peace. You have an eye for beauty, a taste for creativity, and a natural tendency to add a pleasant flavor to all situations gracefully.

Because you seek to understand both sides of a situation, you are a healer and a natural diplomat. True partnerships and romance are on your list of things to do in this lifetime. This number is often called the *romantic number*, and its essence is found in the fashion of the Renaissance and in the artwork of Maxfield Parrish. It brings forces together in harmonious balance, creating a collective bond. You desire to share your beauty with an equal partner because you invariably understand that wisdom comes from the balance and marriage of two opposites.

The number 2 is about creating balance in your life between the yin and yang and with the five elements: (1) earth, (2) water, (3) air, (4) fire, and (5) ether. It speaks of developing the divine masculine and feminine in one embodiment. It is learning to be fierce and tame simultaneously and knowing the right timing of being in alignment with both. It is coming into relationship with others because you have something to offer unconditionally.

You must learn to create healthy boundaries, tend an open heart, and maintain a creative soul because these are your gifts and abilities given to you to work within the frequency of the number 2. Overcoming duality and judgment allows you to perform your greatest accomplishments and offers the freedom to create a life beyond your wildest dreams. Breaking free from any limitations of low self-esteem brought on by codependence is your biggest challenge, but it is necessary for you to mature and grow into the liberty-defined, virtuous person you are designed to become.

Loving and taking care of yourself enable you to love and care for others in a good, healthy way without sacrificing your dignity and self- esteem. It is important that you practice letting go of any toxic emotional habits, such as possessiveness, jealousy, codependency, obsession, and any other emotions standing in the way of connecting with another person. This number suggests forming relationships with others and growing through the higher vision of peace, harmony, balance, beauty, intuition, romance, and partnership in order to bond and connect. The biggest fears for this number are abandonment, betrayal, and rejection.

You must learn the lesson involving being a meaningful part of a group, whether it is a small group, like a family or a circle of friends, or a large group, like a business or a community. You also must learn adaptability, service, and consideration for others.

Golden Cycle: Number 2

You express yourself best by relating to others and are meant for positions of diplomacy and peacemaking. To move toward your destiny, use tact, power of persuasion, and diplomatic skills to help others resolve differences. You find the greatest satisfaction and fulfillment from helping others resolve obstacles.

This is a time in your life to focus on love, relationships, or partnerships of any kind. It calls for balance in all areas of your life. Balancing the feminine and masculine qualities of your nature is an enormous benefit. Reading, writing, creating, and administering beauty to your life are strongly encouraged.

If you have ever wanted to venture into a career involving counseling or mediation, this enlivens a whole new world for you to discover. Practice healthy boundaries and use intuition to guide you toward a spiritual course of action. This is a harmonious number that promises health, love, and a comfortable financial situation. There is plenty of time and money for socializing, spending quality time with family and friends, and pursuing your favorite hobbies.

Opening Cycle: Number 3 (March and December)

The energy of the number 3 resonates highly with the vibrations of divinity, creative expression, and communication (both physical and psychic), adventure, joyfulness, and freedom.

The numerology of the 3 is seen as the most potent and mysterious of all the single digits because of its holy connections (Trinity of the Father, Son, and Holy Ghost), direct relationship with many folktales ("Three Wishes," "Three Truths," "Three Sisters," etc.), and ancient mythology.

You are an extremely empathic and mystical creature with a lively imagination, friendly disposition, and boundless capacity for empathy, even with those you barely see eye to eye with.

You have natural healing and artistic abilities, allowing your creativity to flow unlimited. Because you are introspective and have a unique view of the world, you see things in a highly creative and artistic way. These qualities grant you the process of releasing any emotional tension through self-expression.

Effortlessly adapting to your surroundings is possible when you ground and shield your energy for protection. Visionary individuals like you have unparalleled access to the collective unconscious through clairvoyance and psychic abilities. Kind and gentle, you are invigorated by shared experiences of music and romance. Any relationship with an opening-cycle number 3 is guaranteed to involve deep spiritual exploration.

The tripod was considered by the ancients to be the simplest stable form that people could create. Past, present, and future; birth, life, and death; and beginning, middle, and end are but a few of the trinities, making the number 3 important to hermetic and mystical philosophy. It is a busy energy, representing motion, social activity, and creative ways of enhancing life and experience. If the energy of this number is focused into one thing, there are no boundaries to what can be achieved.

This is a social number, and the energy is easily admired and enjoyed by others. If the numbers were colors, I would splash this canvas with yellow or gold. The way this frequency catches light when the sun reflects on it is uplifting to the soul and opening to the heart. It carries innocence and vulnerability that attract both children and animals in a playful manner. You have the intuition and ability to hear the voices of angels, and much of your talents are channeled through the higher realms.

The number 3 is the vibration for self-expression and creativity. In this cycle, you are here to utilize your emotional sensitivity to bring positive, heartfelt self-expression into the world. Emotional self-expression is sharing authentic feelings honestly and directly and encouraging others to do the same. The emotional connection you feel to life and others generates a rising energy that, once expressed, uplifts everyone around you. You have the potential to revel in emotions the way a butterfly flutters through the air. At the highest levels, you serve as an open channel of loving energy, arousing others toward joy and inspiration and becoming a force of light in the world.

Dynamic Cycle: Number 3

You are passionately sensitive and use your gifts of empathic abilities to heal everyone around you. Although everyone is empathic to some degree, number 3 people are born open and vulnerable to the energies around them and are naturally connected to mind, heart, and spirit, relying on their empathic skills for survival and success in the world.

The symbol for the number 3 is the triangle, connecting mind, heart, and spirit. It is the threefold nature of divinity, and the essence of the triangle is a current of sacred energy belonging to expansion, expression, and communication. There is a real connection between these three attributes when linked, and when this power is charged, the energy is phenomenal, directed creatively through self-expression and shared with others to inspire, teach, or entertain.

You are sensitive and creative, and when expressing yourself, you charm people, whether it is through communicating, writing, speaking, dancing, designing, singing, photographing, drawing, painting, composing, or performing. You have a strong desire to uplift those around you, and your mere presence accomplishes this quite naturally. Expression is your highest achievement, and when it is unleashed, free to unfold, and transformed into what lies within your heart, the beauty is unsurpassable.

You carry pure passion from the sun and are full of light, love, and laughter. The number 3 relates to giving outwardly, to openness and optimism. You are sensitive, intuitive, empathic, and psychic; with all these gifts, it is easy to misidentify them and get confused. Your path is to take each one of these gifts, experience it on a deep and intimate level, express it creatively through feelings of joy, and share it with the world.

Once your soul awakens, you learn to use acute sensitivity, hone astounding communication skills for the good of yourself and others and inherit the gift of divine channel or messenger. Your unique messages are passionately creative, and your dynamic energy drive confirms that you are here to express. Express yourself, because if you do not find a constructive use for your energy outlet, it turns inward and becomes destructive. One way or another, number 3 frequencies must express themselves, and your power of choice is to use it constructively or destructively.

A truly gifted number 3 possesses exceptional creative skills, normally in the verbal realm, writing, speaking, acting, or similar endeavors. Typically, the dynamic 3 cycle offers the opportunity for above-average ability in some art form. Capturing capability in creative self-expression is the highest level of attainment for this life cycle.

The number 3 is the vibration for self-expression and creativity. In this cycle, you are here to utilize your emotional sensitivity to bring positive, heartfelt self-expression into the world. At the highest levels, you serve as an open channel of loving energy, arousing others to joy and inspiration and becoming a force of light in our world.

All number frequencies have their challenges, and this beautiful vibrant number is not exempt. Because of their sensitivity, people carrying the number 3 will hold on to childhood trauma, resulting in long-term low self-esteem and self-worth. Although everyone suffers from past trauma, it is paramount that these individuals heal their wounds and really learn to love themselves before settling down with romantic partners, finding their purpose in life, and feeling truly connected to the outside world. They are here to heal the wounded inner child of abandonment, rejection, and betrayal while healing any low self-worth and low self-esteem that follow these circumstances. If these individuals carry a victim consciousness, it needs to be carefully observed and cleared. Once healed and liberated through taking responsibility for their lives, those carrying the number 3 experience a freedom to live, love, and create in a world that is safe, nurturing, and supporting. They become free to express themselves in whatever modality they choose. This is when the magic occurs and their inner light begins to shine, unveiling the power of their authenticity.

Egyptian numerology states that 3's liberate through the truth; the star wisdom numerology of ancient Egypt describes this number with "The truth shall set you free." It symbolizes victory after a long struggle, after many tests of courage and determination. It reminds 3's that they have the power and blessing to overcome all challenges and opposition. It is an extremely fortunate vibration in a date carrying many rewards.

As the number 3 symbolizes intelligence, knowledge, and wisdom, you can expect many inspiring thoughts to come through you at this time. Most of these ideas are creative and appear to come from nowhere, and this is all possible because of the auspicious power of this number.

Self-expression at this time is at an all-time high because you feel inspired to let the world know who you truly are. This can be done through the arts, communication, humanitarian work, spiritual development, and ambitious projects.

Golden Cycle: Number 3

You express yourself best through the arts. This is a social number, and you have a natural ability to uplift others with your words and ideas. You are encouraged to express yourself through writing, speaking, singing, acting, litigating, teaching, designing, or composing music. It is time for humor, wonder, and spiritual illumination, and all these energize you to stop taking life too seriously.

You are meant to utilize creativity and optimism in life. Part of your job in life is to help other people realize the power of joy, laughter, and imagination. By helping others who may have lost the joy of living learn to appreciate life and live it to its fullest, you find your own joy and fulfillment. Expressing yourself creatively is the key to making this happen.

Your creative gifts inspire and motivate others, and fame is often in the potential future of this vibrant frequency whose highest ability is performance. When you spend time with animals and children, allowing them to assist in tapping into your innocent and vulnerable nature, you improve creative, intuitive, and psychic abilities and get clear direction on where your dreams are meant to take you.

Opening Cycle: Number 4 (April)

Boldness, ambition, confidence, and motivation are some of the attributes belonging to the number 4 individual. These audacious people are a bundle of energy and dynamism who are born to live life on their own terms, often unwilling to compromise on their beliefs, ideals, and dreams.

Strong leadership qualities define you as a natural-born ruler who knows how to take charge of others, and these traits help you become a winner in all your undertakings. You thrive in positions of power and do not just sit around all day waiting for opportunities to knock on your door because you would rather go out and make your luck and destiny happen.

Your self-confidence inspires people, and this amazing tenacity even persists in tight situations. You are a rooted and earthy nurturer; the number 4 is solidly associated with the element of the earth, from which it gains its strength and stable sense of reality.

This is the number for self-discipline, hard work, and service, and we find its beauty in productivity, organization, wholeness, and unity. The opening-cycle number 4 produces the most trustworthy, practical, and down-to-earth individuals, making them cornerstone members of society and businesses. The goal of this term is learning to take direction and following with dedication and perseverance. Number 4's always demand as much from themselves as they do from others—and sometimes a lot more. They have the kind of willpower that others might mistake for sheer stubbornness, but it is not. It is conviction and endurance.

You find a Zen-like satisfaction in performing the simplest of repetitive chores, as you feel closer to Source when you are restoring harmony to an unbalanced situation. You express yourself best by creating energy. You are highly systematic by nature, and because of your unique perspective toward organizations, you thrive in orderly corporate atmospheres. Number 4's make excellent teachers, musicians, contractors, engineers, surgeons, and healers. They work well with their hands and have an innate understanding of structure, design, and rhythm. Their highest potential in life is to invent or create a plan that eases humankind's burdens.

Dynamic Cycle: Number 4

You thrive on routine and order in life, and if stability is not offered, you will gladly make it happen. Being a rock and someone others can count on in the most uncertain of times is one of your endearing qualities. You often do not picture yourself as a perfectionist, but you don't like walking away from a project unless it is finished, polished, and functioning. *Borderline workaholic* and *perfectionist* are both terms competing to define you.

You thrive on being physically strong and athletic, but you also have the empathic abilities and qualities of a healer. Because you have an acute sensitivity and connection with nature and her elements (earth, air, water, fire), learning to strengthen your intuition, applying necessary energy to bring balance to disease, and transmuting planetary discord are major ingredients to your life purpose. Many 4's feel this intense power at a young age but do not investigate these qualities to their full potential until maturity.

Your meticulous sense of structure, stability, routine, and balance offers you all the elements needed to materialize and manifest your dreams. People using this frequency are driven by a methodical way of thinking and viewing the world, enhancing their ability to use foresight and vision to create whatever projects they are focused on. They are known for their strong work ethic and perseverance at being team players, and they are often team leaders.

Family is important, and you may find yourself drawn back to your roots, seeking answers that guide you toward spiritual evolution. Once you have learned the importance of building a strong foundation and growing roots in your surroundings, even when the ground appears insecure, nothing will stop you from fulfilling your passions.

The essence of the number 4 is auspicious and important in our daily lives because we use its dynamic frequency to explain nature's sacred order, and Native Americans agree with this systematic vibration to describe their own spiritual cultural beliefs. There are four winds (dawn, daylight, dusk, and dark), four directions (north, east, south, and west), four seasons (spring, summer, fall, and winter), four major minerals (gold, silver, copper, and iron), four elements (earth, water, fire, and air), four major archangels (Michael, Uriel, Raphael, and Gabriel), and four phases of the moon.

Healing comes naturally to people with a dynamic 4 cycle because they inherently feel a connection to nature. With their meticulous sense of order, they intuitively know what specific cures treat certain illnesses. Their kinship with nature allows them to communicate with the elements and draw on sacred medicines. All this takes practice, of course, but these abilities are available to the 4's who are called into the healing field.

Health can be a fragile topic within the fabric of their lives, and many have issues leading them back to the healing properties within the elements of our planet. Deep down, they possess the inherent wisdom and luminous secrets of the ancient druids who are now being called back into action. They are being contacted by their ancestors to awaken to the self-realization of who they are and the power they keep.

Golden Cycle: Number 4

You express yourself best by creating energy. You are inspired to build, heal, and create from your imagination. During this cycle, you gain motivation to move forward with any plans you have been putting on hold. Either through necessity or by choice, you find yourself working many years longer than most people. Taking care of others affords you a state of contentment and happiness.

The key to enjoyment is found in organization, good management, and practicality. Finding order in life and personal affairs and building things to last support your life toward fulfillment. By taking responsibility, allowing others to depend on your wisdom, and getting things done, you align yourself with your destiny.

If you are highly systematic by nature, you thrive in an orderly corporate atmosphere, and if you continue to be productive in a mild form of routine, this discipline assists you in completing your tasks. It is suggested you learn more about nature and her four elements because this knowledge will teach you how to apply and direct the research toward healing yourself and others. You have the innate ability to comprehend the elements on a deep and profound level while intuitively knowing the language that nature speaks.

Opening Cycle: Number 5 (May)

Number 5 represents the *human* number because of its relationship to the body: five fingers on each hand, five toes on each foot, five limbs (two legs, two arms, and a head), and five physical senses. It is also the number of the spirit or ether element.

You are generous and loyal to people, and you love to maintain relationships after earning a level of trust. Highly caring and compassionate are your personality traits, and you do not play games, because being direct and honest is important to you. Known to keep the inner secrets of those who confide in you, you have the reputation of being a trustworthy and devoted friend.

You are extremely focused, determined, and diligent in your work. Your dedication is endearing, and because of your industrious nature and your ability to stretch yourself to any extent to finish a task successfully, people define your commitment as remarkable.

You are exceedingly kind, nurturing, and protective when it comes to your loved ones, and because of this benevolence, friends and family treasure these innate qualities and find comfort in being with you.

You neither are afraid to wait nor have the anxiety for it. You live life at a slower pace and are patient with your work because you have a deep-held desire to ponder things and consider every move after analyzing it from all angles. You are extremely clear and committed to your actions, and you have the tolerance to wait for results, diligently assessing a project or task to know whether it is worth investing time and money into, and this helps you attain success in most of your projects.

You express yourself best through the movement of energy and are often blessed with numerous talents and abilities and the potential to sustain a couple of careers at once. Number 5 individuals adapt and change freely, as they are free spirits who have a sense of adventure and curiosity about life. They desire to expand their horizons, gaining insights into the lifestyles of other cultures, and have a talent for finding a common ground with nearly everyone they meet.

Your cycle is one of movement—physical, mental, emotional, social, and spiritual. You are always moving and helping other people. You are a channel for Spirit and are known to grasp higher wisdom right out of the air. If you accept your drive for action and seek ways to strengthen your inner core, the accumulation of leadership, balance, expression, and endurance add to your healing source and power.

Dynamic Cycle: Number 5

You are extremely sensitive, intuitive, and observant, and high energy levels put you in overdrive, giving you the ability to stay in motion always. You have a heart of gold, and you desire to use your energy to be of service to anyone less fortunate than yourself. Because this energy is so strong in the number 5, it is not uncommon for these individuals to become healers or physicians of one field or another.

You have a close relationship with Spirit and feel at home in your own skin. Because of this, you are highly adaptable, thriving in challenging circumstances and constant change. Knowing that all you need to survive is a warm heart and a sunny disposition is a key element to your success in life. Nobody can disconnect your union with Higher Source, and your belief in this truth keeps everything balanced in your world.

Dynamic-cycle number 5 people are often blamed for acting impulsive. In several standard numerology reports, this is viewed as a negative trait—something that needs to be corrected rather than understood.

As I see it, your "impulsive" behavior is described by people without intuitive abilities, or else they would know that people like you are acutely intuitive and do not need to go through the same filters as the average person in order to make a decision. Dynamic-cycle number 5 individuals intuitively know when to decide and do not hesitate to pounce on taking action when the opportunity arises.

This is why dynamic-cycle number 5 people go into the fields of frontline warrior occupations: police officers, nurses, paramedics, military persons, firefighters, emergency room doctors and personnel, and the like.

They are quick on their feet when accessing a challenge and do not hesitate to act, especially when it can save a person's life. Using their intuition and open hearts systematically to help others in need makes them excellent healers.

Those of the number 5 express themselves best through the movement of energy, including transformation, change, and adaptation, taking their intuition into the next level, above the standard five senses.

The number 5 energy is the phoenix rising out of the fire. It burns with the flames of divine creation and cannot or will not be contained. It is the fuel driven from the wild horse medicine, transmuting all negativity into pure passion. This type of energy is meant not to be understood, only consumed, and unfortunately, few people define the rhythm and do it justice, because words tend to imprison the true soul journey of this vibrant frequency.

You express yourself best through the movement of energy. You are blessed with numerous talents and abilities and the potential to sustain a couple of careers at once. Number 5 individuals adapt and change freely, as they are free spirits with a sense of adventure and curiosity about life. They desire to expand their horizons and gain insights into other cultures, as they have a talent for finding common ground with nearly everyone they meet.

Your cycle is one of movement—physical, mental, emotional, social, and spiritual. You are always on the go and helping other people. You are a channel for Spirit and grasp higher wisdom right out of the air. If you accept your drive for action and find ways to strengthen your inner core, the accumulation of leadership, balance, expression, and endurance will add to your healing source and power.

Motivation burns like fire in your soul, creating a restlessness deep down in your subconscious and leaving a sense of urgency when it is not directed. Transformation is a fire element and friend to the number 5 who takes the time to learn how to activate its powers. You are intuitive, curious, and wise and have a thirst for knowledge, leading you to reading three books at a time, always. With all your talents, being a healer, artist, or teacher keeps you right on target for the dynamic cycle made for the number 5.

Personal freedom is important, along with speaking your truth without fear of being judged. Allow yourself to pursue your dreams and experience appreciation without attachment. Dare to search out unfounded territory within yourself, break some boundaries, tear down some walls, and challenge yourself to reach new goals. We are never too old to learn something new or undo something not serving us anymore. If you want to be constructive and proactive during this cycle, participate in any cleansing exercises that free up your energy, time, and space.

Golden Cycle: Number 5

There is a lot of movement in your life during this cycle, and you will be traveling, moving, or changing occupations. This frequency supports transformation of any kind, but the highest focus is on spirituality. Teaching and sharing your healing resources are expected. Create from your passions, and savor divine inspiration.

These years are rich with activities, personal freedom, travels, and changes. It is a favorable period to learn, experience new things, find pleasures, enjoy friends, and have all sorts of adventures (love life included). The possibilities for personal alchemy are numerous, and this pushes you toward self-discovery and knowledge.

You are in a number 5 frequency cycle, requiring you to seek, expand, and embrace change. Change is a portal of potential and is a precious opening for a myriad of new ways of being, seeing, and doing things. Growth never goes backward. Change is growth in motion, freedom, and life. Release what is weighing you down and stretch out your horizons. This means the physical and geographical limits of what you think are possible. Break your own mold.

Opening Cycle: Number 6 (June)

You are sociable, adaptable, and talkative and love to be surrounded by interesting people. Being a highly passionate and easygoing being finds you ready for an adventure or intellectual conversation.

You possess a sharp wit and extremely dry, sarcastic sense of humor, but you are enthusiastic and full of life and seek to accomplish new, interesting things. Being highly intelligent, you always have engaging things to say and share. You are curious and inquisitive—ready to gain knowledge and learn new things.

You are one of the most versatile people, capable of handling multiple things at a time and excelling at all of them. Your multitasking ability helps you indulge and balance a variety of projects. Because you are drawn toward a wide range of topics (because of your keenness and curiosity in obtaining knowledge) and enjoy learning new things, you find your hands in different fields and get bored easily.

You love people and believe the greatest expression of your inner divinity is through teaching and guiding others, and you are happiest when you see the positive results of your influence blossom in people.

You have a truly outstanding sense of responsibility, love, and balance. You are helpful and ever conscientious, making you quite capable of rectifying and balancing any sort of inharmonious situation. You are inclined to give help and comfort to those in need and have a natural penchant for working with the old, dying, sick, or underprivileged. Although you have considerable creative and artistic talents, chances find you devoted to occupations that show concern for the betterment of the community.

The most precious lesson for you is learning how to heal yourself with the same love and compassion you give to others. You will deal with relationship issues in this cycle, and the most important relationship is with yourself, the second priority is with the Source of your understanding, and then with other people—in this order!

You are empathic and have a heart connection to all things, which allows you to be a direct channel for healing grace and become the nurturer and caretaker of your family, friends, and community.

The number 6 is the vibration of love, both human and universal. It is the number of the wounded healer. Health issues arise that defy treatment, and you will go to great lengths for a cure but never discover a breakthrough until you stop and say, "OK, God, here I am!" and make a promise to be of service as a healer in some way. As a number 6, you are destined to become a healer or adviser because of your extreme empathic nature.

Dynamic Cycle: Number 6

Throughout the lives of everyone touched, you are the earth mother, or father of the universe, wrapping solar arms around everyone with passionate warmth, brightness, and harmony. You are a lighthouse for divine energy, and your radiance manifests creativity and healing energy to support others.

Self-healing—and being wise to listen to this voice closely— is your inner calling and journey. You know deep down in your heart that you cannot transmit something you do not have. Your love and inspiration are the lingering songs everyone's ears are longing to hear. Focus on the pureness of heart because it always leads and tells you the truth.

The most precious lesson for you is learning how to heal yourself with the same love and compassion you offer others. You will deal with relationship issues in this cycle, and the relationship you have with yourself is the first priority above all others.

You are empathic and have a heart connection to all things, which allows you to be a direct channel for healing grace and healing hands, and you eventually evolve into a nurturer and caretaker of family, friends, and community.

The number 6 is the vibration of love, both human and universal, and is the number of the wounded healer. Health issues arise that defy treatment, and you will go to great lengths for a cure but never discover a breakthrough until you stop and say, "OK, God, here I am!" and make a promise to be of service as a healer in some way. As a number 6, you are destined to become a healer or adviser because of your love and extreme empathic nature.

Besides being the number that reminds us of our connection to the ascended masters, intuition, and the higher realms, the number 6 is a personal message to carve out time for the practice of self-love, which includes installing healthy boundaries.

The number 6 points toward our empathic light workers. They are especially known to assist people in the nurturing and caretaking fields, including the medical field, counseling, dietetics, hospice, and childcare. They are hands-on people in their chosen occupations. They have a strong sense of responsibility to assist the less fortunate and to make a difference in the world.

They often overextend themselves in the nurturing department, and a lifelong lesson for everyone is the development of self-love. So, for this cycle, the theme best served is *nurture ourselves.*

Light workers can be hard to identify because they have many qualities that are common. But for light workers, these traits are more than just preferences because they are traits that drive them from a very core level.

Some of the signs of being a light worker include having a sense of being an outsider; being extremely sensitive; having a rebellious nature; tending toward expression, development, and spirituality; and possessing a strong drive to help others.

There is a high frequency of these old souls throughout our world, and they are light workers simply by helping others, following their guided intuition, and getting involved in social or planetary causes. Other signs of being a light worker include constantly seeing number sequences, finding feathers on one's path, or having the ability to see auras. All these are signs that people are light workers and awakening to their inner truths.

Allow romantic dreams to surface during this cycle and explore new ways to connect with people you love. When your heart and mind are open, creativity sprouts from your imagination and flourishes in your home life and relationships. Take advantage of your many talents, and bring beauty, harmony, and love into every avenue available—even leave room for the unexpected. Bringing more beauty and comfort into your home is splendid for maintaining daily serenity and uplifting your spirits whenever you walk through the door.

Golden Cycle: Number 6

You express yourself best through the balance of energy. An exceptional individual, you are born with an innate talent of uplifting the spirits of others, especially during hard times. You accomplish this through service, art, cooking, music, writing, or one of your many other talents and gifts. Your highest potential is restoring balance to ailing individuals or communities.

This number points to beauty in your home life. Creative domestic qualities surface, allowing improvement to your surroundings. Romance blossoms during this term, or you may want to polish up the relationship you are presently in. Reach out to siblings, children, and extended- family members, reacquainting yourself and connecting with those who contribute to your life.

This cycle is perfect for creating a special place for grandchildren and animals in your life. Be creative by tapping into psychic abilities and expanding your awareness with nature. There are many ways to express your multi-talents and make health awareness a priority on your list of things to do. Volunteer in your community, using your domestic charms to help those less fortunate than yourself.

Celebrate family and all who are encouraged or invited into your circle of friends. Trust your wisdom, love, and truth by sharing with the many people you resonate with, and start a support group, meet neighbors, or attend a community meeting. This is a positive and enriching time to enlarge your cluster of companions by sharing your innate veracity.

Opening Cycle: Number 7 (July)

The number 7 is the holiest and most magical of all the numbers. In Egyptian numerology, this number represents the "Seeker of Truth." It possesses strength, curiosity, and a psychic connection between the spiritual and physical worlds. It is reflective, inquisitive, and always searching for answers behind life's hidden meanings and mysterious manifestations.

The number 7 is auspicious and important to nature. There are seven days of the week, seven chakras, seven notes to a scale, seven colors in a rainbow, seven stars in the Big Dipper, and seven major archangels. Enhanced with the number 7 vibration, you are blessed with an expansive and wild imagination that turns a word into a story in a matter of minutes. It is therefore unsurprising that you are often hailed as a creative genius. You feel extremely happy to share your feelings of love for someone or something artistically through poems or writings and have a strong creative force. Keeping yourself involved in art is a wonderful outlet because you take great pleasure in expressing your visionary gifts artistically.

You possess a supernatural sense of intuition, unique receptivity, and an empathic nature, and you are attracted to those who are also sensitive to their emotions. You have the gift of being able to understand the emotional states and feelings of other people.

Being a reserved, analytical, and peace-loving soul who is blessed with intuition and intelligence, you are connected to nature on a profound level. Your ability to concentrate, learn, and absorb information far outshines those of other numbers, and you excel at all forms of scholastics. Usually, your intellectual prowess, clarity, and foresight of mind are evident to others at an early age.

You are a spiritual number, believing wholeheartedly in the relationship between Mother Nature and science. You possess strength, curiosity, and a psychic connection between the spiritual and physical worlds. Your intelligence and intuition often lead you to being in the right place at the right time.

You are able to excel at any career you choose, as you have the discipline and mental power to master anything in half the time as those of other numbers. Because you are a number 7, your mind works at the speed of light, but this often makes it difficult for others to understand you. Others simply cannot evaluate or analyze information as fast as you can (in fact, some 7's have such quick minds they have difficulty expressing themselves). One of your life challenges is to learn how to slow down and accommodate those of us who may not be as intelligent as you but who may offer you the rewards of emotional support in life.

Dynamic Cycle: Number 7

You were born into higher wisdom, and you celebrate an open mind filled with knowledge, curiosity, and wonder. You have a direct link to Spirit and other worldly realms, keeping you occupied and fascinated in your alone time. You fear that no one could possibly understand your secret world of fantasy, so you keep to yourself and hold your imagination safe in your pocket of dreams.

In your spare time, you love to learn about the holy mysteries, metaphysics, ancient civilizations, the paranormal, and planetary enigmas, and you research these topics endlessly. Somewhere deep down in your soul, you live in solitude with the truth that you are a mystic and a seeker of our universe.

You have a kinship with the wilderness and the elemental spirits. Nature in its true form will never deceive you, and it is here that you practice, trust, and love freely. You are attracted to people who share your passions and are always searching for a twin survivor.

The dynamic cycle of number 7 is to use the gift of channeling higher wisdom and teaching the world what you find to be true in your heart. Although you are not the most social number, it is important that your path leads to your sharing your knowledge with others. All your gifts and abilities make you an exceptionally interesting person to be around. It would not be unusual to find you in the field of science, research, nature, healing, geography, history, or astronomy. Overcoming your fear of being judged by the outside world and putting your faith in the knowledge that both spirit and nature are one are challenging. This is something you were born to do, and deep down, you will struggle until you find your unique outlet that allows you to do this.

You are a genius, psychic, intuitive, and channel for higher wisdom. Your nervous system is overly sensitive, and your path thrives on nature being the ultimate teacher of the universe. Seven is a mystical number, symbolizing wisdom, seven chakras, and the seven heavens. It is our first cycle number, the first seven years of our lives. It is a symbol of birth and rebirth, religious strength, sacred vows, path of solitude, analysis, and contemplation.

You are a reserved, analytical, peace-loving soul who is blessed with intuition and intelligence. Your ability to concentrate, learn, and absorb information far outshines those of other numbers, and you excel at all forms of scholastics. Usually, your intellectual prowess, clarity, and foresight of mind are evident to others at an early age.

You are a spiritual number and believe wholeheartedly in the relationship between Mother Nature and science. You possess strength, curiosity, and a psychic connection between the spiritual and physical worlds. Your intelligence and intuition often lead you to being in the right place at the right time.

Golden Cycle: Number 7

Spiritual awareness, mysticism, and an understanding of the subtle meaning of one's dreams are all common in a 7's golden-cycle term. Communing with, absorbing, and learning from nature are highly effective tools for you. You have been active in your previous years, and now it is time to reflect, meditate, get quiet, and learn how to find silence within the depth of motion. Spirit is asking you to connect, reflect, and possibly dissect parts of your life still waiting to be explored.

You become a channel for higher wisdom when you corral your thoughts and focus your energy. It becomes effortless to be one with Higher Source when your intention is directed through love and gratitude. You are an intelligent, passionate, and creative being, and this is your time to develop a personal system to nurture all three qualities to enrich your soul-life journey and benefit those around you.

You will find your hobby during this period. Follow your inner voice and explore things you are interested in, because during in this cycle, you can succeed in anything you do. Appeal to your inner self and follow the guidance of your heart. This time is associated with meditation, existential thoughts, and personal progress. Your exploration is oriented inward. You need time on your own to think about life, your destination, what you want to achieve, and how you see yourself in your dreams.

Opening Cycle: Number 8 (August)

You are a very caring soul who loves to live the good life and will fight against all obstacles to have everything you desire. You love living life in your own way, on your own terms, and on your own conditions. You are an optimist who sees the silver lining in life and perceives the positive side of any situation you face, preferring to revel in the good rather than dwell over the bad. This affords you a big circle of friends and acquaintances, whom you care for and nurture with your generous nature. At your best, you are courageous and strong with an amazing, protective attitude toward your friends. You care very deeply for those close to you.

You are a popular, natural leader, born with a regal aura and altruistic spirit, often attracting a large following. Loving stardom and always wanting to be a superhero or queen bee for everyone are part of your personality. You work hard in social gatherings, and your natural confidence, intuitive disposition, and desire to please others are popular traits among your peers. You are an inspiring entertainer with a vivacious personality who loves to be center stage, and when you are present, there is never a dull moment at a social gathering.

Your kindness, compassion, loyalty, and protective nature have you feeling responsible for the happiness and well-being of your loved ones, and you will stand up for the underdog every time.

You are very honest, extremely direct, and straightforward with people and will give honest feedback when asked because you do not believe in false modesty and will never speak a white lie just to impress others.

The energy of the number 8 is about manifestation, accumulation, and the attraction of resources or abundance.

The most popular areas in your life are money, fame, and power. The number 8 represents the infinity symbol and refers to energy flow. A powerhouse of energy, you are here to learn to regulate the flow of giving and receiving unconditionally. The central work for you involves contacting your inner abundance, inner power, and inner authority, and when you find these inside yourself, they manifest naturally in the physical world.

If we look at the two loops upright, the bottom circle symbolizes humans or earth linked to Spirit or heaven, acting as a direct channel from Spirit to humans and vice versa. The cycle of the number 8 power is staying fluid by learning to set clear intentions and finding inner abundance. The outside world reflects what is happening on the number 8's inside.

As an 8, you are like a steel rod from the earth to the sky in a lightning storm. You access pure electrical energy when open and flowing, and this allows you to create. The cycle of karma—the idea that we receive what we give—is what you are here to learn, and once you understand and implement it, it naturally grants you abundance.

As an 8, you need to experience inner abundance, power, and respect before you manifest those qualities in the outside world. You are born with a natural source of wisdom, needing to maintain integrity with regard to the spoken word, as well as with money, authority, and fame—you must avoid any kind of abuse in these areas.

It is important that you develop the attitudes, skills, and confidence to understand the laws of material success, such as the fair balance of energy exchange. When you make service the center of your life— sharing money, energy, and wisdom as freely as you are able—you embrace your journey at the most elevated level, combining money and worldly power with the power of the heart.

On an extremely high plane, you feel the inherent abundance of life, nature, and spirit and feel moved to share with those you see as family. Your sense of power or control changes to grateful and loving surrender for a greater authority, higher power, or infinite source, as manifested in the intricate intelligence and web of life as it unfolds.

Dynamic Cycle: Number 8

You are Tiger in the Winnie-the-Pooh series, bouncing with energy and vivacious fervor. You are born with surges of electrical current directly delivered from Higher Source, and this energy heals by mere presence alone. You probably started healing family and friends while you were still in your mother's womb.

As you reached puberty, you started to notice that not everyone carries this type of energy. It is important to keep this portal of energy open, learning to use it to manifest your dreams into reality. This takes years of practice, but the decision to remain open starts now. There will be opportunities and times of challenge when it appears easier to become blocked and reserved, but this only leads to ill health, stagnation, and depression and is not a long-term solution.

Your true power relies solely on your connection to a higher guidance, and everything else is a distraction or an illusion. Your intuition will tell you that your true authority, abundance, and resources come from within you rather than from outside sources, and it is wise to listen to your higher self because many waste a lot of time doing otherwise.

Begin to picture yourself as the infinity symbol upright. The bottom circle is your connection to earth, and the top circle is your sphere to heaven. Begin to practice running the electrical current in, through, and around you, dissolving whatever blocks the flow. Keeping upright and fluid is your magic link to higher achievements in all you do.

Integrity is your keyword. If you are aligned with integrity while giving and receiving in balance, your resources flow naturally, allowing amplification and manifestation when materializing your dreams. Keep your well of dreams open by aligning your intentions and motives with purity of thought and of the highest good for all involved. It is rewarding to remember that money and finances are the equivalence of energy exchange. What flows in must flow out, or else you will create a blockage of resources and abundance.

Evaluate your physical health and increase your vitality by maintaining or expanding exercise and eating a healthy diet. You will want to challenge your physical capabilities, whether through yoga, tai chi, vigorous cardio, aerobics, swimming, dancing, or walking. Celebrate your physical body by adding positive components to your life. The goal is to be healthy enough to enjoy your well of dreams.

Although the power of this cycle points in the direction of finances, careers, and bank accounts, and of empowering yourself as the CEO of your life, do not forget to include your relationships with others as a crucial necessity toward moving forward in life. Take inventory of your family circle and friends, and ask yourself, "Are they supporting me or holding me back?"

The number 8 cycle is a quest for personal power, freedom, inner satisfaction, contentment, and happiness. Within this time lies opportunity to finally do what you want to do, and part of the journey is having the courage to search your heart and soul for what you truly desire to accomplish. If you already know what this is, then you have the advantage to reach it on a much higher level. Seize this opportunity and bet big on yourself.

Golden Cycle: Number 8

You express yourself best by creating prosperity, and you have a natural talent for making money that is unrivaled by those of other numbers. Your highest potential in life is to become wealthy and share your riches with others. This frequency opens the door to strive, accomplish, and succeed in your work and hobbies. Setting goals and working diligently toward them rewards you with many gifts, including authority, personal recognition, and financial success. Work for the sense of accomplishment of a job well done and the simple love of doing what you do, and happiness coupled with success will likely follow.

This is an energetic time of life and ripe for investing. You have the potential for considerable achievement in business or other powerful arenas. You are a pillar of the community who has amassed a prodigious amount of wealth. Use your energy, knowledge, and skills to build something of value for your community. Your creative juices flow when you are inspired, and it is suggested that you direct your flow of energy toward a project that is fulfilling not only for yourself but for others as well.

Take your enormous gift of potential and allow it to storm through your veins. Ask Higher Source how to best be of service. The answers come when your own house is in order. Your health, relationships, and finances sustain a maximum state of balance when you truly serve from the heart. It is only when this flow is blocked that challenges occur or come to surface. This is a universal law.

Opening Cycle: Number 9 (September)

You are blessed with powerful intelligence and are always ready to expand your knowledge reserves. You have a systematic approach to life, leading you to compartmentalize, and what allows you to find solutions to tough problems is your keen attention to detail. You are reliable, organized, and prudent and have an analytical mind that sees things in black and white. You are incredibly talented and give off extraordinary energy.

You appear calm and collected but underneath have a great intensity, demanding to bring order into our world. You need to rearrange your frantic interior beneath the calm exterior until everything is perfect. You are patient with others and have a gift of seeing the good in people.

You are very honest and tell others exactly how you feel without sugarcoating your words, believing that honesty is the best policy, even if the truth hurts. Besides valuing honesty, you are an exceptionally reliable individual who keeps up with commitments. You never let your loved ones down and always give your best to meet their expectations. You are the first to answer the call for help and the last to leave a situation when someone is in need.

You seek perfection in everything you do, from your career to hobbies. Confidence, ambition, and intelligence are necessary components to your character, and your perfection qualities work well with your analytical and practical thinking. You easily find flaws and notice imperfections in everything you do.

You are a natural at problem solving, and you gladly tackle the problems of others. Initially, friends and family may think you are trying to control their lives, but they soon realize that you are analyzing their situations to find ways to help and improve them.

The number 9 symbolizes sanctuary, contemplation, and self-awareness. This true path of the seeker eventually leads to ascension. You have an unquenchable thirst and desire to understand the greater mysteries in life. Your natural tendency is to look within and above for all answers to the questions asked from the mundane world, even going to remote locations to search your soul in the quest for the ultimate truth.

You are rarely consumed with worldly ways because nature is the ultimate teacher for the number 9. This is true not just for pure solitude reasons but for the unlimited lessons the wilderness provides. The life cycle of the number 9 is one of selfless service and the humanitarian way. You use love and inspiration as a drive to solutions. Throughout your life, in this incarnation, you illustrate your spiritual path through deeds more than words. You are all about walking the talk, and honor is a human value you seek to instill within yourself and find in others.

Dynamic Cycle: Number 9

You were overly sensitive and independent as a child, and this is your nature throughout life. You are a truth seeker and hold honesty as a high virtue, next to love. Your empathic nature, combined with a desire toward humanitarian services, often leads into the life work of healing. You are an old soul who was born wise beyond your years, and because of your many lifetimes tapped into higher wisdom, this becomes apparent during adolescence. Many may have spoken with you when you were a child and felt as though they were receiving wisdom from a sixty-year-old sage.

Your soul has prepared you for spiritual evolution by creating circumstances that allow you to achieve higher virtues, such as forgiveness, compassion, unconditional love, and selfless service. Your courage and strength are the guiding forces over the dark night of the soul. The angels and your guides will pull you through some of the hardest times a human will undergo, and eventually, you arrive as a wounded healer, a true leader of humankind, and an artist of true colors.

Number 9's are visionaries, healers, psychics, and artists, as portrayed in the tarot of the hermit, depicting the 9 as a wise old man. One hand bears a lantern of sagacity lighting the way, the other a staff of authority to steady his feet. As he stands in the wastelands, breathing a sigh, the burdens of the shaman, the walker between worlds, sometimes lead to a life of reclusion. That moment of silence is one of prayerfulness when the hermit listens to the voice of the Divine and returns to the world with a message. Number 9's are channels to higher wisdom.

Completion, compassion, forgiveness, and selfless service are a tall order for the number 9, but ultimately, this transforms you into a light warrior and wounded healer. You are the protector, walker of light, and embodiment of integrity, and anyone who stands next to you is guaranteed protection without judgment or fear.

You tend to be reclusive or entertain a hermit lifestyle mainly because you inherently do not want to accumulate more drama or karma in life. Those who walk the dynamic cycle of the number 9 gift the world with sage wisdom and incredible kindness, reminding us that by allowing our divine light to shine, we can change the world. This energy is of the greater good.

The number 9 symbolizes sanctuary, contemplation, and self-awareness. This true path of the seeker eventually leads to ascension. Spirituality cannot abide stagnant water, and you have an unquenchable thirst and desire to understand the greater mysteries in life. You have natural tendencies to look within and above for all answers to the questions asked from the mundane world. You even go to remote locations, searching your soul in quest for the ultimate truth, and will do this several times in your life as necessary to process any new information you have encountered.

You are rarely consumed with worldly ways because nature is often the ultimate teacher for the number 9. This is true not just for pure solitude reasons but for the unlimited lessons the wilderness provides. This dynamic cycle is one of selfless service and the humanitarian way. You use love and inspiration as a drive to solutions, and throughout your life, in this incarnation, you illustrate your spiritual path through deeds more than words. You are all about walking the talk, and honor means something extremely near and dear to your heart.

Golden Cycle: Number 9

You express yourself best by seeking the truth. This term finds you involved in humanitarian causes. You have an innate understanding of human nature, are considerate and compassionate, and are blessed with literary or artistic gifts. Your highest potential in life is to achieve enlightenment.

You are meant to bring charity, beauty, art, romance, and perfection into the world. By living a life filled with generosity, kindness of spirit, compassion, forgiveness, and understanding, you are rewarded with ultimate happiness and a wealth of gifts from the universe. You live your life with the goal of making even the most ordinary things in life lovely and full of beauty.

This is a cycle of life that calls for completion, and you need to examine all areas of life that need closure. This could be in relationships, feelings, events, or projects. You are asked to serve humanity in a big way, and this could be through one of your many creative talents or maybe a new one. Teach, write, instruct, or volunteer your energy assisting the less fortunate. Clean out your closets and get rid of anything that no longer serves you (literally and metaphorically speaking). Learn to forgive, accept, and lead with an open heart.

Dynamic Cycle: Master Number 11/2

Your purpose is to inspire and integrate divine intuition by helping others raise their energy fields. You are here to develop psychic, healing, creative, intuitive, and channeling abilities and to express them here on earth with the power of Higher Source. Your purpose is to always be in touch with self-awareness by learning to trust and use it daily.

This frequency ensures the path to imagination, inspiration, realm of magic, journey of miracles, and manifestation of dream materialization. Tapping into this energy leads you to be a teacher, writer, artist, healer, or psychic reader. The avenues of your purpose are limitless once opened to the magic of the number 11.

Your purpose is toward achieving self-enlightenment and helping others attain a higher state spiritual evolution. It is your ambition and challenge to maintain an eminent quality of light and love. Trusting and developing your intuition serve as a useful guide by directing you toward your true ambition in every situation.

The number 11 symbolizes intuition and illumination and delivers you back to center every time you enter a period of self-doubt or stumble into a pattern of dark illusion. The lower frequency of this master number is the number 2. This energy is more grounding, serving as a connection to others in a skillful manner of peace and harmony. The number 2 is the dominant vibration in this cycle until maturity (forty years or older)—and for a good reason. You need to transcend the lessons of the number 2 for the activation and magic powers of the number 11 to manifest. The highest quality of the number 2 is learning the balance of divine masculine and feminine within yourself. It is also about overcoming judgment between dualities meaning developing the properties of acceptance in all areas of your life. This is a tall order and often takes a lifetime in and of itself.

Spirituality, enlightenment, and self-awareness are the winds under your wings in this incarnation. You were born with a high-energy field, and your challenges are to maintain these qualities in a world of doubt and confusion. In other words, family, friends, and community will not always support you, so it is important that you seek out like-minded people to guide, reinforce, and maintain your quality of purpose. That said, your focus is to use your intuition and creativity to inspire others to reach spiritual heights that you can envision but they never dreamed possible. This assists in raising the consciousness of all souls seen and unseen.

You came here to be a true artist and an example of right living, and this includes the passageway through the dark night of the soul. You are a wounded healer who overcomes your challenges because only then can you become a true teacher, leader, and healer of humankind.

Golden Cycle: Master Number 11/2

You express yourself best through spirituality. You are a channel and conduit for spiritual wisdom and feel a great need to transform the world with your visions. You have an innate spiritual strength, an acute awareness of others, and a positive transformative effect on people's lives. Your highest potential in life is to lead others to enlightenment.

You are encouraged to inspire people through creative abilities that may not have been available to you before this time. Intuition is heightened, and psychic insights surface to serve you in times of need and solitude. You have the opportunity to travel to interdimensional realms and visit with beings from the other side. During this cycle, the potential for self-awareness and illumination skyrockets, and your connection with Higher Source will be a natural communion of great strength.

Use available resources during this cycle to assist the less fortunate in various ways. Writing, artistic talents, hands-on healing, and remote-viewing techniques are only a few abilities you can share with the outside world. The power of the 11 cycle is a magical time and promises great rewards for those courageous enough to call on its source.

Dynamic Cycle: Master Number 22/4

Building castles in the air and pulling them down to manifest expression here on earth is a gift bestowed on master number 22. "Building castles in the air" is a phrase used to illustrate the acute use of imagination those of this number have available to them. It comes from the number 11 doubled, allowing for strong intuition, inspiration, illumination, and awareness. The 22 is known as the master builder because when the two are added together, it equals the number 4.

Four is the number of productivities, stability, and order. The double 2 gives it immense power and strength, allowing it many possibilities, such as dream materialization. You are the action number, and when you stay focused on your dreams, the universe pulls together resources, aiding in materialization. Your power is so strong you can feel the energy pulsing through your veins when becoming motivated to the cause of your desires.

This number is similar to the master number 11 cycle and the path of the wounded healer. The magic properties of the master number 22 become mature around the age of forty and older. Until then, you are learning the energy of the number 4, as it must be mastered before evolving into the power of the elusive number 22. You will feel the undercurrent of this master number rumbling under your feet all your life, encouraging you to move forward and onward.

You have all the abilities of the master number 11 available to you, as well as the gift of manifestation. In this cycle, you must stay focused, learn to channel higher wisdom, and build your grandest castle that serves the greater good. The master number 22 contains the superpower of dream materialization with incredible perception and intuition, access to a dream or vision world, and the ability to ground it down into reality systematically through a structure of rounded tangible effort, work, and action.

You get intuitive insights guiding you like the North Star in the physical world. Be the dream-materialization architect by taking your vision and solidifying it in the physical world so that all of us can enjoy a new foundation and way of experiencing living life. You uniquely create your own reality and must dare to follow your North Star and be different. You are the trailblazer, trendsetter, and master builder, possessing special gifts, strengths, and weaknesses others do not have. You have extra protection from the angels and a green light to go and manifest!

Whatever you think about is sure to become a reality; therefore, it is exceedingly important that you choose your thoughts carefully. If you are willing to work for your desires, you will achieve enormous prestige, success, and fame. You are endowed with exceptional powers and have a unique talent for manifesting ideas into the realm of reality. Sometimes you display what looks like insensitivity, but you are just extremely focused on your goals.

Like the master number 11, you are destined to enter the dark night of the soul during your lifetime, and this is entirely necessary to achieve your destiny.

You were given the strength and tenacity to overcome all diversity, so all setbacks only make you stronger and wiser. You are creative and imaginative, and your dream world is connected to Spirit. You knew from a young age that you came here to do amazing things, and power surges when you start to manifest your ambitions, as others are drawn toward your charisma, courage, and perseverance. This only reinforces your drive forward to succeed with the projects you encounter and for those still waiting to be discovered in your fluid imagination.

Understanding structures fascinates you, and through maturity, you learn that the foundation in all areas of life need to be solid to create long-lasting bonds, whether in relationships, business, or buildings. Nature is your ultimate teacher and friend through adventures and discoveries. Her elements hold not only the secrets to inner and outer healing but also the properties of sustaining life itself, and somewhere deep down, you know this is the true foundation you have been searching for.

Golden Cycle: Master Number 22/4

You express best through building a better world and are called the *master builder* because of your capability to manifest great changes on the earthly plane. You do this through the construction of empire, whether social, financial, or religious in nature. You are a master of manifestation who knows how the power of a negative thought or image destroys potential. You fulfill your highest potential by bringing spiritual ideals into everyday reality.

This is the 11 doubled, and the main difference is that the energy is so strong that it must be released. Elevens have direct access to Higher Source, and the 22's must use their energy to manifest in the material world and find a way to help humankind. Using creative forces and deep intuition leads you to being spiritually guided in developing the resources needed to fulfill your mission here on earth.

You are energetic and methodical in nature, and while this puts you steps beyond the normal population, Higher Source always has the upper hand in matters. There are truly no limits to what you can achieve during this cycle in your life. Be mindful of your intentions, because you are surely going to materialize what you put your focus toward. Your whole life has been groomed for this moment, so rejoice and create directly from your heart memory.

Dynamic Cycle: Master Number 33/6

You are friendly and love interacting with people and animals. You possess high empathy, compassion, and mentorship qualities, promoting your protective and nurturing expression. Experiencing high imaginative abilities is common, along with possessing creative talents and finding solutions when in pursuit of a goal or manifesting an ideal. There is a devotion to family, which extends beyond biological and in- law relatives to include the neighborhood or an entire geographical area.

In this cycle, you will have prominent nurturing skills, become a great adviser, be devoted to loved ones, take love seriously, and prefer long-lasting marriages and a warm stable home. You are able to cure others' wounds because of your compassionate soul, and you understand that every situation is a lesson—this is why it is not unusual for you to become a great teacher.

You are happy when entering a trusting and warm union that allows you to contribute the skill of nurturing, and you are always ready to give advice, counsel, or offer assistance. You radiate a protective and sympathetic concern for others' lives and well-being, and this gives people the impression that you are a confident and trusting person.

You dress modestly and are not interested in fashion, although you have your own style and understand what is harmonious and appealing. Sometimes you place family or others ahead of yourself while neglecting your personal appearance. In most cases, you dress for comfort and prefer to avoid dramatic, exotic, or flamboyant styles because you have other, more important things to accomplish than personal adornment.

You were born with open, clear sensitivity to the spirit realm and empathy toward the outside world. Being a direct channel of grace, you are optimistic in most situations. You have many creative gifts, and because you are an empathic person, it is important that you express yourself by releasing inward energy.

You have a double 3 influence, which exercises intuition, psychic talents, and creative talents in the arts, and this emphasizes interest in writing, painting, singing, or performing. All these are forms of expression you can share with others. Communication is an important aspect of this master number and a vital form of releasing stored-up energy.

All your gifts can swing the pendulum into self-doubt and low self- esteem at times but remembering who you really are at your center keeps you anchored. Part of your challenges and lessons is to form healthy boundaries so you know which energy belongs to you. This is about growing into the power of your master number and maturity. The good news is that the 33 has balancing and grounding tendencies.

The number 6 represents universal love and harmony. Once you have appeased the pendulum, your greatest achievement will be to channel pure creative energy from Spirit and to communicate or express yourself and teach others. You are a master teacher.

Golden Cycle: Master Number 33/6

Besides being a channel for Spirit, you express yourself best by teaching others. Your superpowers are communication, expression, sensitivity, and creativity.

You have a childlike wonder and curiosity that is filled with joy, love, and beauty. Your intuition and empathy keep you connected to your friends, family, and community. We may find you in a healing, advising, or creative field, where caring for or nurturing others predominates your other skills.

You are a triple dose of sensitivity, empathy, and artistic abilities. Having these qualities leaves you open and vulnerable, so you need to learn how to set boundaries and protect yourself.

The main challenges with the golden cycle of the number 33 is to learn self-love on a deep and profound level before loving and healing others, always knowing that you cannot transmit what you do not have. It helps remembering that everything on the outside of you is a mere reflection of what you hold near and dear on the inside. Healing always starts with self.

Thirty-three is the number of the master teachers of our time and the time before. This vibration brings to light the statement "We are the ones we've been waiting for." Yours is the path of divine expression and power of the spoken word. You guide, heal, direct, and restore people with altruistic powers and rather high energy. You have the gifts of imagination, dream materialization, and illumination, which are the accumulation of all three master numbers combined. Einstein said, "Imagination is everything. It is the preview of life's coming attractions." Your golden cycle includes raising awareness and consciousness, uplifting, and bringing joyful loving energy to the world. By balancing your 33 energy here on earth, you are bringing the world into a state of balance.

Golden Cycle: Master Number 44/8

The superpower of the master number 44 is in enterprise and business toward the cycle of sacred order. You have the ability to attract resources in perfect harmony with nature and the environment. I envision you as a pure electrical current of energy balancing commodities with the perfect flow of giving and receiving.

Your primary gift is in offering stability and correcting establishments that are corrupt by exposing truth, repairing injustice, and rebuilding sacred structure. You bring natural order through communication, communities, and institutions. Because of your ability to attract accumulation, flow, and balance, your path is to assist the world of business by bringing it back to right and high order. You have extraordinary talent for maintaining organization and envisioning complex and unreachable ideas, and you are fully capable of following through with your ideas. The number 44 combines the strengths of the master numbers 11, 22, and 33. Not only can you foresee and implement what is needed to create something monumental; you also want that bigger picture to help humankind in a big way. You are insightful like the 11, creative like the 22, and nurturing like the 33, and you refuse to be intimidated by any challenges along your path.

The number 44 cycle finds you hardworking, disciplined, systematic, professional, trustworthy, and composed both physically and mentally. You are deeply spiritual, wise, and inspirational to many people. It is believed that this number is working through the process of reincarnation and ending its cycle. You are here to help yourself and others advance to the next level of incarnation. You have the power of dream materialization and can break the chains of the material world by lifting the veils of illusion to see reality.

This number is the vibration of self-discipline, abundance, and success through balance. Balancing between two worlds in the areas of family/work, spirit/earth, and emotions/logic, 44's need to build a strong foundation in all of them. Balancing issues come up around the number 8, and the number 44 is about business building and how it can be related to benefit present and future generations.

The master number 44 is known for magnificence and manifestation. You are a master architect and alchemist whose leadership skills transform ideas and structures into powerful, life-altering accomplishments. Your lesson is to go beyond the hard work of the mundane and perceive each moment as a creative challenge. The obstacle to be defeated is perfectionism in order to gain humility.

Cycle Number 12

I call the twelve-year cycles *the portal years* because it is during these years that the universe offers guidance through whatever means possible, including lessons, challenges, and opportunities, to lean us toward emotional maturity on our soul-life paths.

Not all twelve-year-cycle events are devastating, but they are meant to change the courses of our lives on an emotional level. We all have free will, but some of us do not learn the lessons we came here to learn. Some of us will struggle, some of us will succeed, some of us will take our lives, and some of us will not even remember that anything significant happened to us between the ages of eleven and fourteen. No matter what happened to us, it is our responsibility to extract the lessons from our lives and advance closer into the love and light that we truly are. Those of us who suffered a tremendous personal loss are wounded healers, and those of us who struggled for years after the first twelve-year shift or who may be struggling still are known to have entered the dark night of the soul. Both events are given only to true spiritual warriors.

This cycle symbolizes the gateway to opening portals from the other side, as well as opportunities to advance spiritually. The number 12 is a transportation number and is used to travel from one dimension to the other. It signifies power and change from development, sequences, and patterns. It ignites one's destiny, and in some cultures, this is the age when a child begins adulthood. It is the age when a boy or girl becomes a man or woman. Puberty is established, and not only does the body go through changes, but the outside world triggers events that form and change an individual's future life. The number 12 has the frequency of the number 10 plus 2. It is the number for the rite of passage in many cultures and represents twelve months, twelve hours, twelve disciples, and so on.

The first twelve-year cycle is called the transition cycle and can include divorce within the family, death, relocation, illness, marriage within the family, new birth, assault, or an environmental shift (fire, earthquake, hurricane, tidal wave, etc.).

Age 12—Portal to maturity
Age 24—Portal to invincibility
Age 36—Portal to temple of knowledge
Age 48—Portal to spiritual freedom
Age 60—Portal to destiny
Age 72—Portal to dream time
Age 84—Portal to immortality

Cycle Number 28

This cycle is referred to as the *Saturn return* and is symbolized as the transformative cycle. Immense power is distributed during these cycles that allows us to tap into dramatic changes in our lives. Introduction to the major occurrences and clarification toward the reasons we are incarnated are as follows:

Age 28—Introduction to life purpose
Age 56—Introduction to life destiny
Age 84—Introduction to life dimensions

CONCLUSION

The paths of wounded healers are determined before birth by their higher selves, guides, angels, and the karmic board. The wounded-healer path is the highest honor and privilege that a human can endure in one lifetime.

This journey is summoned only for advanced old souls and those strong enough in their spiritual directives to hold the immense energy needed to complete their missions.

Wounded healers must undergo the dark night of soul, which triggers the awakening process. When wounded healers evolve through their challenges, they have the power to free hundreds of thousands of people taken hostage by their own shadows, heal generational wounds, clear future legacies for their children, and heal their own karmic debts.

The history and teachings of Egyptian numerology begin with the story of Pythagoras, including his many lifetimes as a wounded healer and the gifted insights of decoding number frequencies uncovered through his research, experience, and connection to Source.

The healing modality of Egyptian numerology includes decoding our birth dates and names to discover our paths, karmic lessons, purposes, and destinies; the initiations and virtues hidden within each number frequency; the timelines and cycles of our lives; and the importance of raising our energies to extract our highest possibilities and outcomes.

The personal ascension is our primary purpose, and its teachings originated long before Christ was born. Ancient wisdom has resurfaced as a result of the veils of illusion lifting, which in turn restores our inner truths and reasons for incarnation.

Egyptian numerology's prime purpose is to help us restore the memory of why we came here and to ascend to the next level of consciousness. Overcoming our personal challenges is paramount to those of us with a calling to be a healer, whether through hands-on healing, art, writing, music, photography, composing, inventing, or teaching.

The lessons of a wounded healer vary with each individual, but if we follow our challenges, they always lead us to the same destination: self-love, compassion, and forgiveness.

Every person, place, event, or circumstance reflects a version of ourselves, whether of the light or the dark. Unless we learn to face our own shadows, we continue to see them in others because the world outside of us is always a reflection of the world inside of us. Showing ourselves forgiveness, compassion, understanding, and patience as we venture through the process of traveling from the third dimension to the fifth helps the transformation and development toward our new earth.

Understanding our place in the world, why we are here, and where we are going is what Egyptian numerology strives to achieve. We encourage, confirm, and challenge all light workers to uncover and discover their soul-life agreements and manifest their destinies.

Although our paths are sovereign journeys, we are never alone. Come forward and shine your light in our world, step into your brilliance, and perform your magic.

My next book is called *The Miraculous Healer: Becoming a Conscious Creator*. The primary focus is on our personal year numbers, universal year numbers, conscious-creator year numbers, repeating numbers, and more. Thank you for taking this journey with me.

To your love and light and living it!

Sara

You can contact me through my website at:
www.egyptiannumerology.org.
Private chart readings: https://bit.ly/ChartReadingEgyptian.
Join our community Facebook group:
https://bit.ly/EgyptianGroup.
Email: opentothe5th@gmail.com.
Ninety-day mentorship program:
http://bit.ly/About90DayMentorship.
Follow my blog: www.egyptiannumerology.blog.
YouTube: https://bit.ly/SaraBachmeierYouTube
and Instagram: https://www.instagram.com/sara bachmeier1/

ABOUT THE AUTHOR

Sara Bachmeier, born and raised in Santa Barbara, California, experienced her first spiritual awakening at fourteen and became a devoted seeker. Bachmeier earned an associate degree and owned a pre-school. She teaches and holds an array of certifications, including Egyptian numerology, women's self-defense, postpartum depression, children's literature, complete cellular mind body alignment and activation, and complete cellular soul memory clearing. Bachmeier lives in Arizona where she conducts workshops, writes, and works with clients.

Visit her at www.egyptiannumerology.org.